Beyond MESSY Relationships

Praise for
Beyond MESSY Relationships

"Most books about marriage use couples as their data. This book is different. Judy Herman, a couples therapist, is the client in her own book. In it she reveals her painful journey through a messy marriage to an ordered and joyful one. To illumine her journey and to inform her readers, she grounds her experience in the latest marital theories and research. Couples and therapists will benefit from reading it."

—Hendrix, PhD and Helen LaKelly Hunt, PhD
Getting the Love You Want: A Guide for Couples
harvilleandhelen.com

"Not many therapists would risk the personal and professional vulnerability Judy has by sharing her journey through her own messy marriage. But she shows us all how important it is that we stop blaming and focus on doing our own work of forgiving, healing and growing. Her research and professional insights were spot on. Learning to take deep breaths of AIR, her formula for awareness, intentionality and risks is a tool that we won't soon forget. Reading this book will give you a new lens to see your next steps and gives hope for your future."

—Leslie Vernick, Counselor, Relationship Coach, International
Speaker, Best-selling Author
The Emotionally Destructive Marriage
leslievernick.com

"All living is relationship. Relationships are messy when we imagine a self in relation to another rather than awaken to the truth that there is no self without other and no other without self. Judy Herman's *Beyond Messy Relationships* is a divine invitation to realize this truth. The book is told through her eyes. Let it resonate in your heart."

—Rabbi Rami Shapiro, Author
The Sacred Art of Lovingkindness
rabbirami.com

"In *Beyond Messy Relationships*, Judy Herman has done something remarkable as a marriage counselor in applying the wisdom of her practice to her own relationships, through all their travails and triumphs. With grace and courage, she has answered the question that we have all wondered at one point another: What's my therapist think about all this? And there is so much to learn in the answer."

—Mark Lukach, International Best-selling Author
My Lovely Wife in The Psych Ward
marklukach.com

"Judy does what every great leader must do: she goes to the hard places before asking others to do the same. Through her empathy and vulnerability, she gives us all permission to be ourselves in this insightful book about relationships. If you want to wake up to a deeper and better way of living and relating to people, read this book."

—Jeff Goins, Bestselling Author
The Art of Work
goinswriter.com

"Compelling and insightful. *Beyond Messy Relationships* takes you on a powerful journey of vulnerability, adversity, strength, and hope. The insights Judy shares from her personal life and as a mental health professional combine to share true wisdom about the challenges and opportunities we encounter when we open our eyes and minds to the signs around us."

—Nick Pavlidis, Author
Confessions of a Terrible Husband
nickpavlidis.com

"I was not able to put *Beyond Messy Relationships* down and read it from beginning to end in one sitting. I was touched by Judy's authenticity and masterful threading together of therapist and woman. This was an amazing story that I will feel for a very long time to come."

—Alice Taylor, Business Coach
yourtayloredlife.com

"Judy Herman has written a book that allows the reader into the most intimate workings of the human heart. But not only that. She also shows us how to work with and through life's big dilemmas. A book of great honesty, as well as help, it was written for us all."

—Marion Roach Smith, Author
The Memoir Project
marionroach.com

"I am a man who has experienced messy relationships. In these pages I crossed over the chasms of divorce, mental health wellness, children of divorce, narcissism, codependency, faith and God's divine invitations that appeared as choices in each part of the story. The gem is the through line that ties back to the Authors marriage to a man who has Bi-Polar Disorder. The reader can make choices that lie within each divine invitation. Author Herman has shared her strengths, limitations and passions that have kept her moving forward and for sharing her vulnerability, this book should be lauded."

—Tom Dutta Founder and CEO KRE-AT, Author
The Way of the Quiet Warrior
Motivational Speaker and Producer/
Host of The Quiet Warrior Internet Radio Show

"Who wants a counselor or therapist that is open about their own struggles and messy relationships? I do! You will see yourself in the personal stories and dances shared in Judy's book. More than that, you will learn from her experience as an authentic woman and a compassionate counselor, the kind of attitudes and skills that will enable you to thrive in the middle of the mess."

—Ken Davis, Storyteller, Comedian, Author
The Secrets of Dynamic Communication
scorreconference.tv

"Seldom do I come across a book that is as practical as it is engaging. In *Beyond Messy Relationships*, Judy shares her story of disappointing relationships while inviting the readers to address their own. As a licensed therapist, it's clear she knows her stuff. But what comes through most in the book is her honesty, transparency, and love. If you are struggling to untangle your *messy relationship* you'll be moved and inspired by this book.

—Phil Ayres, Pastor, Author
Flannel-Graph Jesus: More Than A One-Dimensional Savior
philayres.me

"I started reading *Beyond Messy Relationships* as a favor to my friend Judy, but quickly found myself lost in the pages. Instead of reading from an outsider's viewpoint, I was drawn in and became the patient, nodding my head in agreement many times. Much healing can happen when we find those who validate what we have personally experienced. So much of Judy's story will resonate with the reader because she has lived through many of life's difficult moments. Thank you, Judy, for being so transparent on the pages of this book. You have exposed some very real and raw emotions for us, the readers, and we are grateful!"

—Sheila Harper, Founder and President of SaveOne
saveone.org

"Judy Herman is in touch with the relational needs of men and women who are struggling to make their connections [especially in marriage] work... in spite of the dysfunction and division observable virtually everywhere you look today. With rare humility and transparency, the author of *Beyond Messy Relationships* shares from her education and experience to both refine the thoughts and rekindle hope in the hearts of what will be a growing audience of readers seeking perspectives and strategies for relational health."

—Dr. Ken Idleman
VP of Leadership Development for The Solomon Foundation

"Judy Herman brings understanding of interpersonal issues and emotions that accompany them. These extend beyond marriage issues, though that is the context in which they are presented. Do you have children? You need this book. A boss? You need this book. A friend? Ditto. Highly recommended to anyone who has a pulse and does not live in a cave on a mountaintop."

—J. L. Callison, Author
Rotund Roland
jlcallison.com

"What I so appreciate about reading Judy's journey is her authenticity, her vulnerability, and how I, as a reader, can find hope. Forgiving and remembering are powerful tools in the journey and Judy portrays that with grace and love. Thank you, Judy, for showing us the dance."

—Nancy Booth, Spiritual Director
nancyboothcoaching.com

Beyond
MESSY
Relationships

Divine Invitations to
Your Authentic Self

Judy K. Herman, LPC-MHSP

NEW YORK

LONDON • NASHVILLE • MELBOURNE • VANCOUVER

Beyond MESSY Relationships
Divine Invitations to Your Authentic Self

Published in New York, New York, by Morgan James Publishing. Morgan James is a trademark of Morgan James, LLC. www.MorganJamesPublishing.com

Unless otherwise noted, all Scripture passages are taken from the New King James Version of the Holy Bible. Copyright © 1982 by Thomas Nelson. Used by permission. All rights reserved.

New American Standard Bible, (NASB). Copyright © 1960, 1962, 1963, 1968, 1971, 1972, 1973, 1975, 1977, 1995 by The Lockman Foundation.

ISBN 978-1-64279-321-5 paperback
ISBN 978-1-64279-322-2 eBook
Library of Congress Control Number: 2018912252

Cover Design by:
Rachel Lopez
www.r2cdesign.com

In an effort to support local communities, raise awareness and funds, Morgan James Publishing donates a percentage of all book sales for the life of each book to Habitat for Humanity Peninsula and Greater Williamsburg.

Get involved today! Visit
www.MorganJamesBuilds.com

TABLE OF CONTENTS

PROLOGUE

I spend the first moments of most mornings on the front porch swing. It's become a place of reflection, prayer, and a hot cup of coffee.

After my husband's second psychotic episode from his bipolar disorder, I had to write this book. Yet it was a risk for me to share my private life. Most of us mental health therapists don't. Instead, we keep the counseling process a mystery. But I believe otherwise. There are times I've said to my clients, "If you knew about me what I know about you, you might say, 'And why am I seeing her as my counselor?'"

Some couples show me their ability to create tenderness between them. That gives me hope that Joe and I can do the same. And other days I come home from the office with a greater appreciation for our connection. Counseling couples has helped me gain resolution about the marriage I couldn't save.

Whether it's couples or individuals, I'm privileged to have entered the sacred spaces of those who trust me. Without them, I would not have the courage to write. And I know this story is not mine alone. I've heard too many within the four walls of my office not to notice similar themes and relationship dances.

None of the scenes in this book reflects any one certain client or couple I've worked with. Names, ages, sexes, and roles have been changed. Some are a combination of several people in one character. With that anonymity, I seek to reflect the truth of my experiences while honoring those who are represented. I've also changed the names of my former husband, classmates, doctors, therapists, health care workers, and colleagues. My stories may be unfamiliar landmarks to some readers, whereas others will recognize themselves in the saga. Be assured that I write from our common conditions and experiences. Years of counseling others have taught me, more than I'd know otherwise, about our unique yet similar human struggles and triumphs. And as a result, I believe we all share similar journeys of our relationship messes.

Reading any book is never a substitute for professional counseling services. Each chapter begins with a "psycho-educational" blurb before getting into the scenes. I encourage you to read at your level of readiness. Intense emotions have been stirred from readers I've never met. And it's important for all of us to care for our emotional well-being whether we're reading a murder mystery or an inspirational novel.

Of course, writing this book has taken me places I didn't expect. It has aroused stories from my journal entries that I had previously forgotten. Many have been cut to provide a concise flow to my theme of divine invitations beyond the messes.

This book is not only about shattered dreams, traumatic marriages, or psychotic episodes. It's about all of us becoming aware of our purpose beyond our messy relationships. It's about widening our vision to recognize invitations for our authentic journey. As we begin to notice, we won't be able to deny the formula of breathing in fresh AIR (awareness, intentionality, and risks).

I wholeheartedly believe three things about relationships.

1. All relationships go through seasons of messiness.
2. Divine invitations come through those in-between spaces of our messes.
3. We cannot know our authentic selves apart from the mirrors of our intimate relationships.

Shall we experience divine moments together as reader and writer? Would you take the time to honor your value, dignity, and worth as you dive into the story? You might want to enjoy a cup of hot tea or coffee as you make space to nurture your soul.

The gentle rocking of the front porch swing that holds my body weight reminds me of life's movements. It's a picture of the security and energy God provides for each of us. Whether your relationship is like the swing, or you're on a roller-coaster ride, may this book help encourage you to say yes to those divine invitations. Your true self is waiting to be known.

Chapter 1

SACRED SPACE

*First there is the fall, and then we recover
from the fall. Both are the mercy of God!*
—Lady Julian of Norwich

My previous client had just left my office, allowing a short window of time for me to write a few case notes. A new client sat in the waiting room a few feet beyond the closed door.

The counseling office has been like sacred space to me. I took time to equip it with a gurgling fountain, lighted candle, and soft Indian flute music. The atmosphere always reminds me of the work I've felt called to do as a mental health therapist. It's holy ground because it's an emotionally safe place for my clients to be brave and real. But the time in between that client and the next didn't feel so sacred.

The hospital number showed up on my phone, and I answered. "This is Judy."

"Mrs. Herman, this is Dr. Morgan."

"Oh, thank you for calling, doctor." I'd been calling the nurses' station between my sessions. Although relieved my husband was in the hospital getting the care he needed, I was on edge. Every hour with a client was a gift of disconnect from the terrifying fear of the last five days. I switched mental zones to face the reality of my situation.

"I just saw your husband," the doctor said. "This is going to be a hard case." Wait. I didn't expect this. Since Joe had gone to the hospital, I was confident he'd be zapped into reality. He was finally getting around-the-clock psychiatric care. Couldn't he take the right medication, get the sleep his body needed, and refresh his brain? My Joe would come back. The man who adored me and danced with me and partnered with me.

I felt lightheaded and almost sick to my stomach. My ability to create a peaceful environment instead became a place of raw despair. I reached for a pen and notepad and settled on the couch. This was supposed to be sacred space for my clients. Instead, I was the one who needed to be brave and real.

I listened to the doctor. "I'm sorry to say that your husband is refusing all medications. He believes they're poison."

"Oh." Silence held my warm tears.

"I'm sorry. This is the first time I met your husband. We had a good connection."

I took a deep breath.

He tried to make the situation lighter. "Your husband said he knew thirty times more than I did about psychiatric medications."

We chuckled.

"I'm not surprised," I told him. "He's bragged about knowing more than most. Didn't know if you were aware that he's led bipolar support groups for years."

"Yes, I've heard great feedback from patients we've referred to his group," the doctor said.

Ah! This psychiatrist knew of Joe's positive impact on the mental health community.

"What is his prognosis at this point?"

"Several days without medical care doesn't help. We hope he'll agree to medication in the next few hours. If he sleeps, we may be able to stabilize him by the weekend."

The doctor waits for my response.

"What happens if he keeps refusing? He can be so stubborn in his right mind. Can you give him an injection sooner rather than later?"

"We avoid forced treatment as long as we can. It's best for him to comply."

"It's been over five days now! Won't he get worse?" I heard my voice get louder.

"It's true, the longer he's psychotic, the more challenging his recovery. Again, it will be better overall if he agrees. We'll need to wait."

"What if he doesn't?"

"The only way we could force treatment is to present his case before a judge. He would be assigned an attorney to represent him. But let's not worry about that now. We'll take it a step at a time."

I couldn't speak. Nor could I believe what I had just heard. None of the breathing techniques I taught others worked for me. I jotted notes with a shaky hand but could barely comprehend anymore.

The doctor asked if I had support and encouraged me to take care of myself. He would give me an update tomorrow. My thoughts raced, and I reached into my desk drawer for my powder compact to freshen my red-hot face.

Weeks before, I had noticed Joe's heightened energy and religious awareness. I thought it was a spiritual awakening. Over a period of several months, he had become more active. He facilitated the local DBSA (Depression Bipolar Support Alliance) group.[1] He attended events and trainings to become a certified peer recovery specialist.[2] I was so proud of his accomplishments as a mental health advocate and spokesman. He initiated and helped organize a citywide mental health awareness event. He had gained the respect of community leaders. And he was well connected with the clergy at our church. He attended weekly pastoral staff meetings and was about to be ordained as a lay minister.

But I didn't think any of this was out of the ordinary. His heightened stamina and influence made me proud to be his wife. I thought, *That's my man, and isn't he awesome?*

Joe spoke openly with me about his manic episodes in the past. His stories seemed as intense as Kay Jamison's in her book *An Unquiet Mind*.[3] Jamison is an international authority with severe bipolar disorder. Our class discussed her memoir during my graduate studies. I believed Joe had conquered the worst of his illness just as Kay Jamison had with hers.

As a mental health counselor, I had minimal experience of severe bipolar symptoms. I had been a crisis counselor who did assessments to treat "troubled teens." For me, trauma work was intense and dark. I could only handle a year of it while establishing my new counseling practice.

---

1   Depression and Bipolar Support Alliance is a non-profit organization with local chapters providing support for families, friends, and those with depression and bipolar disorder: https://www.dbsachattanooga.org.

2   Certified peer recovery specialists, who have core competencies with lived experiences, impact peers beyond other mental health professional services: https://www.tn.gov/behavioral-health/mental-health-services/peer-recovery-services/peer-recovery-services/certified-peer-recovery-specialist-program.html.

3   Kay Jamison, *An Unquiet Mind* (New York: Vintage, 1996). You can find her at https://www.hopkinsmedicine.org/. Her Facebook page is: https://www.facebook.com/KayRedfieldJamison/.

Joe was honest with me about the onset of his illness as a high school graduate. West Point, the United States Military Academy, had accepted him for admission. He had a bright future ahead. But he didn't go. His first manic episode changed the arc of his life.

He shared his dramatic stories and experiences of being a psychiatric patient. He told me of his parents' heartache and how helpless they felt. He was almost shot for stealing a police car during one of his grandiose episodes. Another time he got past security at the NASA space center when the *Challenger* space shuttle was ready for takeoff.

Some of the forced medications put Joe in a catatonic state. He was mistreated and beaten by police and tech workers in the emergency room. When he was nineteen, his psychiatrist cried in front of him after hearing of the physical abuse he had endured. The mental health system was brutal then and is still flawed now. His proper diagnosis and compliance to treatment came much later in his life.

I was amazed at his resilience as he shared more throughout our slow-developing friendship. He was brilliant and lived with a life-threatening illness. Yet he was a man of substance and depth. My trust in him grew because he was brutally honest with himself. He gave me every opportunity to run in the opposite direction. I was attracted to his intense personality and fun-loving steadiness.

Then our friendship reached a point where I needed to make a decision. Would I choose to grow emotionally closer to him? We enjoyed our dancing, hiking, bike riding, and hanging out. He was becoming my best friend. I didn't know if a romance or possible marriage was even a wise consideration.

My training was out of town for a certification program of a particular relationship therapy I later specialized in. The experiential learning helped me understand the anatomy of my first marriage, which ended in divorce. I became aware of my chemistry with Joe. Although he never pressured me, our friendship was progressing into a slow romance. I reflected about the intention of our relationship.

In my time of reflection, on the paved walkway in the park, I prayed in silence. Then I felt a physical presence of peace around me. It was one of those "divine invitations"—those moments that have the power to turn our lives around. We're aware of a bigger story and purpose.

> "It was one of those 'divine invitations'—those moments that have the power to turn our lives around. We're aware of a bigger story and purpose."

I began to realize how Joe's character, stamina, and faith were part of his bipolar journey. And it was part of him. He was one of few men I'd ever known who could be his authentic self. He didn't try to impress me. Instead, he embraced his imperfections as gifts from God. I learned to embrace him. But I had never experienced his stories in real time.

I'd never known anyone more generous and kind and loving as Joe. He loved life and lived it well. He had depth of character. And he loved to dance. He respected me like no other man had. We grew into a spiritual bond and friendship neither of us had known before. We were great partners. We both had teachable and kindred spirits with our love of learning and outdoor adventures.

By the time we talked about marriage, it had been over a decade since his last episode. We both were cautious to make sure we were a good fit for each other. His self-care was crucial if we were to be together.

Joe's doctors and therapist affirmed the unlikeliness of another episode. His diligence with his treatment rewarded him with years of wellness. He was consistent in attending support groups, therapy, and doctor appointments.

Through the drama of his stories, Joe never mentioned that psychosis was part of his diagnosis. Both of us must have put too much trust in the other. He assumed I was aware of the psychosis part. After all, I was a mental health professional. But I assumed that I could trust his insights about his past.

"Don't be alarmed if I just need to leave for a while and go out to the mountains for a few days," he said. I thought I understood what he'd need in the unlikely event he'd have another manic episode. And I trusted his long-term wellness.

"Oh," I said as a naive girlfriend.

"The best way you can help is to just let me go and be in the woods by myself. And I'll be back."

His being in the woods and camping along with his beloved dog, Pup, was part of his recovery at an earlier time of life. But Pup had since been transported to dog heaven. And with Joe's take-charge personality, he briefed me on how I was to respond as his wife.

He had been a single man most of his adult life. That's why his agreement to attend a marriage conference every year was so vital to me. How could I expect him to take on the role of husband to a woman whose life was saturated with relationships? Not only was I a professional counselor, but I had four nearly grown children and a grandchild. We were opposites. And he didn't have the drama of an ex-wife or children.

I felt more secure when we said, "I do" as Joe agreed to attend marriage enrichment events with me. We attended a few before the phone call with the doctor in my office.

———————

I pushed too much and ignored his stress. A rare opportunity I didn't want to miss came up. A well-known marriage expert would be at a conference within a thirty-minute drive to the next town. I booked a hotel room and paid for our conference tickets.

"But I'll be speaking to a group of therapists on Saturday afternoon," Joe said. His TV interview about the mental health event provided opportunities to promote his DBSA group.

"We can do both. I can stay for the second day and count it as a business event in my work with couples." He reluctantly agreed, and we drove separately to the marriage conference.

I left in plenty of time to relax in the hotel room and wait for Joe. Then I received a strange phone call. "This is Bondsman so-and-so. Your husband asked me to contact you."

"What?" I said. *This has got to be a prank call*, I thought. *Who would play such a practical joke?*

"Are you Paul Herman's wife?" he asked.

"Yes, he goes by Joe," I said. I was still skeptical to disclose more.

"Well, he asked me to call you and bail him out."

"What?" I said. "Who is this? You must have the wrong number. My husband is meeting me to attend a marriage conference."

"Yes, that's what he said, ma'am. He is in jail and wants you to bond him out."

Joe had been speeding at 110 miles an hour on the highway. I couldn't understand. But I picked him up at the jail. I still believed he could be influenced by attending the marriage conference with me. Listening to this speaker's message would soften his irritation toward me. But after a restless night of sleep in the hotel, Joe left early for his speaking engagement. I went to the event to take in experiences I could share with clients. By the time I got home that evening, it was too late. Days later he required mandatory admission[4] to the psychiatric hospital.

When I got off the phone with Dr. Morgan, I remembered that long walk in the park when I decided to get closer to Joe. I hadn't imagined any scenarios like this during my relationship training.

---

4   Mandatory inpatient treatment is involuntary admittance to a hospital when a person is out of touch with reality and may be in danger to themselves or others.

Instead, I dried my eyes from the shock of what the doctor told me. I took long, deep breaths and prayed out loud. "Oh, Lord. Please help. Please, please, God. Help me now." Joe was my husband, not my client. I was supposed to be the well-composed counselor, but I was falling apart as a wife.

With trembling hands, I looked in the mirror of my powder compact and put on my lipstick. I practiced my smile, hoping I covered the red splotches on my neck and face enough. I needed to look like a professional counselor.

I opened the door of my office and walked down the hall to greet my new client. She avoided eye contact, and I wondered if she were more anxious than me. My world faded and I entered hers. We walked into the sacred space of my office. It was my safe place with the lighted candle, gurgling fountain, and soft Indian flute music. But it was her turn to be brave and real.

Chapter 2

AWARE OF AWAKENING

Awareness is like the sun. When it
shines on things, they are transformed.
—Thich Nhat Hanh

Divine invitations are moments of awakening. It's like waking up from a dreamy state after a solid night's sleep. As we open our eyes, we realize the images in our minds were dreams instead of reality. Then we become aware of the present moment.

Yet most of us function in our everyday lives in that dreamy state. Overcrowded schedules, busyness, technology, and stress keep us from being aware. We live in automatic thoughts, attitudes, and relationship patterns. And when we become aware of divine invitations, we can move beyond the autopilot setting in our lives. Increased awareness is necessary for our authentic journey.

Those awakenings can be traumatic, like the doctor's phone call. That's what I faced while in the sacred space of my counseling office. Like jolts of electricity, they feel scary, dramatic, and overpowering. No one would consider such a time as a "divine invitation." Yet it woke me up to a different level of awareness.

Sometimes we notice divine invitations right away. Other times we don't notice them until years later. And, of course, some people tragically will never notice. But those invitations come from a loving God who securely holds us in both the light and darkness of our authentic selves. Our journey toward awareness is to align with that reality.

We get misaligned through messes in our marriages. Most conflicts with couples I've seen come from unresolved issues dating back to before they were nine years old. That makes our childhood stories worth examining. Personal history holds awakenings that can help us get beyond the messes.

The stories we remember give us clues about our authentic journey. Movement and patterns in our messy relationships are like movement and patterns in the dances of our early relationships. Increasing self-awareness emerges from the mirrors of those closest to us. And, for me, writing in prayer journals is where I've learned to make sense with some of those relationship messes.

"Sometimes we notice divine invitations right away. Other times we don't notice them until years later. And, of course, some people tragically will never notice. But those invitations come from a loving God who securely holds us in both the light and darkness of our authentic selves."

My earliest surviving journal is the one I wrote in while living in Belgium during the summer of my junior year of college. I tried combining fine arts class requirements with missionary tasks. Textbook readings, cathedral visits, and art gazing at the Louvre interfered, so I dropped the course. Instead, I played my guitar, socialized, and lived as a missionary. This was not my only unrealistic expectation.

It wasn't until two decades later (in my mid-forties) that I resisted my diagnosis of adult attention deficit disorder.[5] But the psychologist said that my intelligence quotient, school history, and computer tests confirmed I had a strong case of it.

"How could I have earned all A's in my graduate degree program if I had ADD?" I asked the psychologist.

"You've had to work ten times harder than those who don't have it. It's like running a race with a broken leg," he said. I agreed to treatment thinking it would clean up my part of the marital messes. I was unaware of my phenomenal staying power and heightened energy. For some of my family members, it was too much.

The *Diagnostic and Statistical Manual of Mental Disorders*[6] wasn't around when I was a child. And some of my adult relationships reminded me of my second-grade teacher. She got irritated with me when I tried to be good. She said a firm "Quiet" to the whole class. But she looked directly at me.

---

5   The current diagnosis is now ADHD (attention deficit hyperactivity disorder), which I address later in the book. Edward Hallowell, MD, and John Ratey, MD, give more insight about the adult diagnosis in their book *Driven to Distraction* (New York: Simon & Schuster, 1994), http://www.drhallowell.com.

6   *Diagnostic and Statistical Manual of Mental Disorders* (DSM) clarifies descriptions and categories to help trained mental health professionals provide treatment plans for individuals with mental disorders. Its first publication in 1952 has gone through various revisions: https://www.psychiatry.org.

Dance of Distractions

There was another time I looked out the window instead of following along in my social studies textbook. My teacher called my name since it was my turn to read aloud. My face was warm and my hands were sweaty.

Ears throbbing, I wanted to crawl under my desk. Then she said, "Kathryn?" The next student was ready and smarter than I.

A time before that, I stood next to my dad's coffin with my mom at the funeral home. She held my baby brother on her left hip and stroked my dad's hair with her right hand. He was twenty-nine when he was diagnosed with liver cancer and died six weeks later. Along with this traumatic loss, I learned ways to make sense of my world. We all relate to those closest to us in patterns. We master certain ones to handle the harshness of life. The patterns are like dances.

Dance of Silence

I started first grade in the shadow of my third-grade sister since our small country school didn't have kindergarten. Jackie told me what to do and how to act.

On picture day our mom dressed us in freshly ironed lookalike dresses. I waited in line along with my class, my hair combed with a barrette amidst the curls. When it was my turn, I smiled at the camera while the man behind it tried to make me laugh. Then our class lined up for recess.

Jackie's class waited their turn in the hallway for the bright lights and camera pose. When my class passed hers, I had dirt on my knees, sweat on my face, and wrinkles on my dress. The barrette in my windblown hair was about to fall out.

"You're not supposed to get messy before pictures," she scolded. "Mom's going to be mad at you." I wasn't quick enough to tell her I already had my picture taken. But she was older and knew more than me. The dance steps of silence were natural moves.

Dance of Not-Good-Enough

After my dad died, my mom, sister, brother, and I moved from our rural town to the suburbs. I went to a bigger school with modern classrooms, newer desks, and smarter kids.

Jackie and I didn't pass in the hallway, and I got nervous when my teacher looked over my shoulder. At the end of the year, she told my mom I needed to repeat second grade. My reading skills weren't good enough. Along with the silence steps, I learned the dance of not-good-enough.

Dance of Shame

"You're eight and only in the second grade?" kids would say.

"Yes. I was held back." I tried being honest.

"You flunked!" They laughed at me and pointed their fingers. "You flunked," they said over and over again. I wanted to hide.

I faked being a year younger during the school year. But in Vacation Bible School and summer church camps I was honest about my age, though not the grade. I learned to put up a façade to ease the shame of flunking the second grade. That's when I learned to master the dance of shame. All those dances required a baseline belief of "others know more than me."

Along with learning more dances and ways of relating, our family grew to include a stepdad and another brother.

Dance of Secrecy

My family's biggest move among many was to another state into an old plantation-like farmhouse. The yard was filled with huge pine trees. A certain tree with long branches was wide and high enough for a pretend living room. The pine needle carpet and staircase branches were perfect for our imaginary playhouse.

A large barn, a tire swing, an old shed, and a small pond with lily pads accentuated the two-story house that had been "in the family" for eighty-five years. It was perfect for our family of six. The owners took immaculate care of preserving the historic home. They allowed an outdoor dog but refused to rent to a family with children under the age of five. My youngest brother was three, and our German shepherd's name was Schultz.

It was like a fire alarm. When the landlord showed up unannounced my mom would say, "Quick. Hide Troy." Our fourth-grade class was reading *The Diary of Anne Frank*.[7] When I thought of my family hiding my brother, I pretended the landlord was a Nazi soldier.

Dance of Persuasion

My bedroom with pink calico walls looked like the inside of a Victorian dollhouse. The coordinating bedspread, headboard, and white Ethan Allen dresser aligned with my true self. I didn't share it with my bossy sister. And the Beach Boys sang my feelings in the song "In My Room."[8] I received their album and a record player at my ten-year birthday party when my school friends came to celebrate. I loved to play music.

With a handheld mirror, I faced the opposite direction of my dresser mirror. My long golden blonde hair reached my waist. It was silkier and wavier than I thought. I wasn't aware of what others could see unless I looked at my back using those two mirrors.

---

7   Anne Frank, *The Diary of a Young Girl* (New York: Random House, third printing, 1991). To stay in the drama of my story, I intentionally wrote *The Diary of Anne Frank*, even though the title is *The Diary of a Young Girl*.

8   The Beach Boys, "In My Room," 1964, https://www.youtube.com/watch?v=bV-dWhYklqE.

It was a struggle to get tangles out after washing it. And I began to complain about having headaches. One day my mom said to me, "Judy, wouldn't it be nice to have a pixie haircut? Wouldn't it be easy to take care of? Maybe that's causing your headaches." I thought about it but got distracted playing house in the big pine tree.

I saw magazine pictures of Twiggy,[9] the popular skinny model who made young girls like me want a short haircut. Since mom was good at the dance of persuasion, she made the hair appointment. After all, others knew more than me.

We entered the salon with chemical smells and rows of ladies sitting under large helmet-like dryers. I sat in a swivel chair while the stylist draped a black nylon cape over me. She ran her fingers through my long golden blonde hair, saying something like, "My, you have such pretty thick hair."

My mom answered for me. "Yes, we're concerned it's causing her headaches."

After a wash and a thorough rinse, the stylist wrapped my hair in a white terry cloth turban. I switched chairs to sit at her station facing the large mirror.

The stylist asked, "So you want a pixie today, honey? Won't that be cute on you!"

I muttered an "uh-huh." My dance of silence synchronized with the dance of persuasion. Besides, I was just a kid. And she snipped away and swiveled me in the direction of the old ladies under the hairdryers. I looked down and saw gobs of my blonde wavy hair on the floor. She brushed away the loose hair on my shoulders and swept away the same hair on the floor. I looked at my new self in the salon mirror and smiled.

We left the salon and drove home. I went up to my room and played my Beach Boys album. While they sang "In My Room," I saw another

9   See what Twiggy looks like now: http://www.twiggylawson.co.uk/index.html.

image staring back at me from my Ethan Allen dresser mirror. My long hair was gone. I threw myself on the bed and cried. My mom came up when she heard me. "Oh, honey," she said. "What's the matter?"

"My hair is gone!" I said through my tears.

She hugged me. "Oh, I thought you wanted your hair cut. You said you liked it when we left the salon. Don't you remember?" She reminded me that I looked like Twiggy and how the kids at school would want their hair cut like mine. When I dried my eyes, we stood side by side in front of the mirror. "Look at how cute your hair is! Don't you feel lighter? And you'll really like it when you wash it again."

"Maybe you're right." It felt lighter, and I got used to it.

"And it will grow back, Judy. I think it's pretty on you."

Dance of Rejection

The next day I surprised my teachers and friends as if I were the new girl again. "Do you like it?" they asked.

"Yes. I do like it." Then I began to worry they didn't.

While on the swing during recess, I heard others on the monkey bars in a sing-songy tone with the tune of "Ring-Around-the-Rosie." They changed the words to sing: "Judy Welch is ugly because she got her hair cut." Another one said, "She looks like a boy." I didn't like my haircut anymore. My hair grew back, and I kept a distance from friends.

Dances We Learn
Dance of Distractions
Dance of Silence
Dance of Not-good-enough
Dance of Shame
Dance of Secrecy
Dance of Persuasion
Dance of Rejection
Dance of Resilience

Dance of Resilience

I left childhood behind along with treehouses and playgrounds. In junior high, I became a cheerleader and wore my hair in pigtails. Those uniforms and pompoms gave me identity along with my long wavy blonde hair. I learned the cheers, chants, and moves to "where there's a will there's a way… (clap) … Believe it… Hey."

I was more than Jackie's little sister. Instead, I was the popular cheerleader at school and the pious Christian at church. I graduated a semester early from high school so I could catch up from flunking second grade. Then I enrolled in a Christian college seven hundred miles from home. The same dances showed up in various relationships in my roles as a college student, a new wife, and later as a young mom.

Chapter 3

AWARE OF PERSONAL HISTORY

When I was a child, I spoke as a child, I
understood as a child, I thought as a child; but
when I became a man, I put away childish things.
—1 Corinthians 13:11

One of my mentors, Dr. Dan Siegel,[10] has given me practical tools to help clients understand interpersonal neurobiology. He defines mental health across various disciplines, from psychology to biology, as connections between and among parts of the brain. Simply put, horizontal integration is the connection between the right and left hemispheres. Those who have highly developed left-brain

---

10 I first met Dr. Dan Siegel in July 2014 at the Siegel-Gottman Summit in Seattle. As a clinical professor of psychiatry at UCLA School of Medicine and director of the Mindsight Institute, he has written several books and provides clinical training for counselors and mental health professionals: https://www.drdansiegel.com.

hemispheres are more logical and rational. Whereas the right hemisphere is open to creativity, curiosity, and new ideas.

Vertical integration, on the other hand, has three major areas. The main idea is for neurotransmitters to access various parts for well-being.

I use Dr. Siegel's hand model of the brain[11] to explain how conflicts and escalation erupts. Holding up my hand, I explain how the reactive parts include the brain stem, represented by the wrist as the lower and primitive part of the brain. It only knows danger or safety. It cannot differentiate between self and other, or past and present. Subconsciously, it communicates, "I'm going to die if I don't do something." In a millisecond it reacts in fight/flight/freeze mode. It's the only brain reptiles have. Then I hold up my rubber lizard and remind them that we act like reptiles when we try to out-yell the other. Or when we do the pursue/distance dance.

Then I fold my thumb over my palm and say, "My thumb represents the limbic system. That's the part that moves toward pleasure and away from pain. Those who struggle with addictions or have low coping skills will highlight this 'old' part of the brain. It's also called the mammalian brain, which mammals have."

When I fold my fingers over my thumb as a fist, I explain, "My fingers represent the gray matter, or executive functioning of the brain. This part is both rational and creative. It can differentiate between past and present along with self and other. It has ability for insight and meaning.

"When we trigger each other, our reptile brain takes over." Then I open my hand to demonstrate lack of connection. "You could say we lose our tops when we react. There are a few neural connections in those instances. But if we take three or four deep breaths for about ninety seconds, we help our neurotransmitters to connect." That's when I close my hand in a fist to show how the three parts touch.

---

11   Dan Siegel, *Aware: The Science and Practice of Presence* (New York: Penguin Random House, 2018), 130. He describes the hand model of the brain.

Another dimension of vertical integration is learning how to remember our stories with new understanding and compassion. Growing awareness can give us mature meanings from our childhood experiences. While gaining insights with increased awareness, we have the ability to act less like reptiles and more like humans. We can show up as mature adults in our relationships rather than react like children. We can have the freedom to identify our relationship dances. And we can begin to recognize divine invitations.

"Growing awareness can give us mature meanings from our childhood experiences. While gaining insights with increased awareness, we have the ability to act less like reptiles and more like humans."

First Divine Invitation

The organist played while the congregation sang verses of "Just as I Am."[12] Hearing more about God's wrath than His love, I walked the red-carpeted aisle of our small Baptist church with sweaty hands and shaky knees as a nine-year-old. It was less frightening than dying and going to hell.

The pastor's wife guided me through a prayer, and I accepted Jesus into my heart. While I blew my nose and dried my tears, she asked, "Do you know that Jesus forgave all your sins?"

"Yes." I nodded, and she smiled. My shoulders relaxed.

"And He's forever forgiven you even when you don't feel like it. The Bible assures us in Romans 10:9 *that if you confess with your mouth the Lord Jesus and believe in your heart that God has raised Him from the*

---

12   Charlotte Elliot, "Just as I Am," (1935), https://www.hymnal.net/en/ hymn/h/1048.

dead, you will be saved. And that's what you just did. So you don't need to worry about feelings."

I nodded again.

First Diary

I started writing in my pink-and-blue diary with flowers and peace signs. The mounted metal lock and flimsy key made me think it was secure. As a fourth grader who liked a boy in my class, it became a treasure of secret desires. My diaries could handle all my feelings and understand me like the Beach Boys did. When I grew out of diaries, I took organ lessons. But I wanted to play the piano. I saved every dollar I made from my first job to match my parents' other half for a console Everett. I played for congregational singing and youth events at church. Music touched deep places in me with the inexplicable feelings that emerged during adolescence.

I never tried drugs, but I was curious about relationships. And I learned a prayer to dedicate my life back to Jesus. I was assured that feelings didn't affect my salvation. And I memorized Psalm 103:12:

As far as the east is from the west, so far has He removed our transgressions from us.

First Semester

I left my piano at home and took my guitar to college. My virtuoso grandpa helped me pick a Brazilian acoustic and taught me singalong chords when I was seventeen. Instead of serious studying, I played a few tunes.

"Didn't you read your syllabus?" my roommate asked. I was behind on about seven weeks' worth of daily readings. There was no way I could catch up.

"No. I didn't know I was supposed to." I had become Mark's fiancée weeks before and only planned to attend one semester with fun classes. I didn't want to miss an adventure before getting married. And becoming a college girl was the way to do it.

My high school romance with Mark began when I was a freshman cheerleader and he was a blond-haired, blue-eyed, hardworking farm boy. He didn't play sports, but he was a macho man with muscles. His family was Catholic and mine was Baptist.

I was supposed to witness to this "lost" family. So Mark and I pretended we weren't having sex. My dance of denial kept me from considering birth control. Along with adolescent hormones, the surge of excitement, adrenaline, arousal, and risks produced more guilt than I could handle.

First Engagement

Familiarity, immaturity, and shame kept us bonded. My only choice was to marry Mark because of all the secrets we shared. I couldn't marry anyone else. Even though I was the pious Christian at church and naive girlfriend at school, he knew me as sensual, sneaky, and sexy.

I wore his engagement ring and signed up for fun college classes like bowling and art. My energies went into social life and a "pure" image. Then I'd come back and marry Mark as promised.

New campus life[13] made me aware that I did have choices. I gained clarity about my small world and wondered about dating other guys. No one needed to know my past. I could be a "secondary virgin" and start dating with integrity. I wanted the confidence I saw in other students.

I tried to pray and reason through my conflicting heart and mind. I didn't tell her the whole thing, but my resident assistant helped me realize that I did have choices. It was a risk, but I needed to break up with Mark.

---

13   I chose to go seven hundred miles from home to a small Christian liberal arts college in the buckle of the Bible Belt South: https://www.bryan.edu/about/.

One day I stood on a grassy hill of the campus during a festive student event. I felt a gentle breeze and saw colorful kites moving in rhythm with the wind. I was more than certain that I'd regret marrying Mark. I'd miss out on dating other blond-haired, blue-eyed guys. They weren't simple farm boys, and I didn't care about their muscles. But they all had adventurous lives.

They loved learning and had ambitious goals. Some were missionary kids who grew up on the other side of the world with cultures I wanted to experience. Others had foreign accents and were skilled at team sports. And I wanted to try out for cheerleading. The world was bigger on that small campus. I felt more a sense of belonging than I ever did in high school. Mark didn't fit anymore. Besides, I felt smothered in the relationship. But those kites moved with the wind. And I needed to move too.

A few days later, the dorm hall was quiet. It was time. I had a handful of quarters for the payphone by the stairwell—the most private place while others were in the cafeteria for dinner. I dialed his number. One by one I put coins in the slot. After a few rings, the call went something like this.

"Hello?"

"Uh, hi, Mark…whataya doin'?" I said.

"Oh, nothing. Just waitin' for you to call," he said.

My insecurity spoke. "I…I'm sorry…but I need to tell ya something." My tears took over, and he was silent. "I…I…can't wear your engagement ring anymore." There was a long pause of static.

His fear spoke next. "What do ya mean? What's goin' on? Are ya breaking up with me?"

After more static, my slow whisper said, "I'll give the ring back to you when I come home for spring break. I'm sorry." The words didn't come out as I rehearsed them a million times in my head. I put more quarters in the slot while we listened to the distance. We said our last goodbyes. I hung up the phone and sat on the concrete steps, and the cinderblock walls echoed my groans.

I walked back to my room and grabbed a towel with just enough time before my roommate arrived. A warm shower cleansed away my guilt along with grief bigger than the breakup. I dried my body and dressed the "real" Christian girl that I'd become. Then I sat at my desk and read through every detail of the syllabus.

Just as we didn't talk about my dad's death, I ignored the grief with Mark. Gradually, I learned the dance of achievement with steps of denial.

I heard someone say, "If you don't find your mate during your college years, it'll be harder later on in life. Where else will you be around peers who share your values?" Marriage was the next step. The common joke was that female students pursued their MRS degrees. Men pursued their professional development. The only proper "career" a woman sought was teaching. So I majored in Christian education. College would be the best years of my life since I had wasted much of high school.

It wasn't a different school or a pixie haircut that made me the new girl. My single college self walked into the student center on a Friday night where several students were playing round-robin ping-pong. Anywhere from ten to twenty players gathered around the table. Each took their turn one at a time. They picked up the paddle to volley the ball back to the other side then quickly placed it down for the next player to pick up before the ball returned. Laughter, energy, and bumping into each other made it high-adrenaline fun. Some slammed

"We can show up as mature adults in our relationships rather than react like children. We can have the freedom to identify our relationship dances. And we can begin to recognize divine invitations."

it fast. Others gently pinged. Through cheers and giggles, personalities emerged unhindered from the boldest to the shyest of players.

It was my third awkward date with blond-haired, blue-eyed Stuart Buford from Africa. If it wasn't for his sexy British accent, I wouldn't have been attracted to him since he was the most socially awkward guy I ever knew. My friends assured me he only lacked experience. He had no sisters and was new to the US, having grown up as a missionary kid. And I was fascinated with a bigger world beyond my small town.

During that date, we played round-robin ping-pong. On the other side of the table, I noticed a guy whose name was Richard. I only knew him as one of the soccer players on the varsity team. We caught each other's glances. But he was with his date, Kelly Coolidge. Through laughter and energy, neither Stuart nor Kelly noticed the flirtatious eye contact between Richard and me.

Days later, as I walked from the cafeteria across the student center to my next class, Richard approached me and said, "Uh, I know you don't know me, but I'm wondering if you're planning to go to the party that Coach Reid's having for soccer players and cheerleaders."

"Maybe," I said. I had recently made the cheerleading squad. Stuart Buford was also a soccer player.

"Well, if you're going, do you want to go with me?"

"Aren't you going with Kelly?"

"No. Will you be going with Stuart?"

"No, he hasn't asked. I guess I could go with you."

"Okay, then. Would you like to take a walk after supper tonight down the hill? Just to get to know each other before Saturday?"

"Sure." We took our walk that evening. But at the party, we both felt awkward at being seen as a "couple." Romance developed in the midst of soccer games and cheering squads.

My mailbox was eye level among rows of hundreds of others. It was always exciting to see a letter from home when I looked through the glass door of #2045. I unlocked it and noticed Richard's handwriting on the envelope. The first note was a casual thank-you-for-a-nice-time. Many more followed, progressing to romantic cards and love notes. We enjoyed special events, hayrides, roller-skating, and concerts. We dated, and he graduated. Then I became his fiancée.

Through one engagement to Mark and the other to Richard, I wasn't aware of my hunger for the man I missed as a child: my dad. I wasn't aware of how my family of origin influenced my choice of romantic partners. Both fiancés were the age of my older sister with whom I learned the control/silence dance.

But I'd never again have the opportunity to travel overseas as a single woman. And being a summer missionary was the way to do it. Then I would be a bride and finish my four-year degree.

Chapter 4

AWARE OF ROLES

The first step toward change is awareness.
The second step is acceptance.
—Nathaniel Branden

Awakenings, faith, and early stories affect romantic connections. Our relationship dances help us move toward pleasure and away from pain. This is a universal part of our humanity.

We learn ways to protect ourselves from harsh realities before we can make sense of our world as children. For me, I distanced myself from kids on the playground. That kept me from the pain of rejection. But to continue distancing beyond childhood creates messes in marriage and other close relationships. Also, it keeps us in a small frame of reference about ourselves. In short, what works for us in childhood doesn't work for us in adult relationships. Awareness is the key to getting unstuck.

Along with our individual dances, the metaphor applies to partnered ways two people relate. Our unaware minds are attracted to what feels familiar. That explains why we have "chemistry" with some but not with others. It could be that our caregivers or siblings provided the contrary moves that made our synchronized steps comfortable. For example, my older sister was bossy. And I believed others knew more than me. I was good at silence and comfortable with controlling partners. We could flow in the silence/control dance. My conservative faith, distractions, and beliefs of not-good-enough drew me to partners who were masters at persuasion. Together we moved fluidly in the submission/persuasion dance.

"Our roles in life are designed to increase awareness. And, for most of us, becoming a spouse and/or parent brings greater awareness. That's why weddings and births are such sacred times."

Beyond choosing those with opposite dance steps, partners can be complementary in the same steps. The secrecy/pretend dance is one both partners can synchronize. Another version is the shame/façade dance. When marital messes get worse, some couples keep up the rejection/distance dance. But few learn how to do the resilience/belonging dance.

Our roles in life are designed to increase awareness. And, for most of us, becoming a spouse and/or parent brings greater awareness. That's why weddings and births are such sacred times.

Throughout my growing-up years, authoritative preachers empha- sized messages of certainty. "Do you know for sure that you're saved?" That absolute answer came from the song we sang in Vacation Bible School.

Yes, Jesus loves me. Yes, Jesus loves me. Yes, Jesus loves me, the Bible tells me so.[14]

As an adolescent, I heard two gospel truths from youth leaders. Number one: be sure you're going to heaven when you die. Number two: the next most important decision you'll ever make is who you'll marry.

After breaking up with Mark, I locked up my sexual past just as I locked up my first diary with the flimsy key. Except the secret box was in my head. And I was certain that God removed my sins as far as the east is from the west.

College was the time to choose a life partner. Our values would be the same. I was ready to get my MRS degree along with my bachelor's. Richard and I kept dating and laughed at each other's jokes. I cheered at his soccer games, and we played round-robin ping-pong.

At times I forgot all about the secret box. But other times it got my attention. One of my girlfriends had a secret box like mine. We advised each other to keep it locked. Then she left in the middle of the semester, and I never heard from her again.

Even though I considered it, I couldn't unlock it for Richard. He told me his bride would be a virgin. Since I was skilled at the shame/ façade dance, I was intentional not to miss my college years as the time to find a husband who shared my values.

I sat next to Richard's parents in the gentle breeze on that sunny day for the outdoor graduation ceremony. Each graduate said words of gratitude or quoted Scripture upon receiving their diploma. When Richard's name was called, he received his diploma. Then he stood

---

14 "Jesus Loves Me" was first written as a poem by Anna Bartlett Warner to comfort a dying child in the 1960 novel Say and Seal, written by her sister, Elizabeth Warner. William Bradbury added the tune in 1962: https://en.wikipedia.org/wiki/Jesus_Loves_Me.

behind the podium and spoke his words of thanks after quoting Proverbs 31:30-31.

Many daughters have done well, But you excel them all. Charm is deceitful and beauty is passing, But a woman who fears the Lord, she shall be praised.

Everyone knew he was talking about me. But since his mom was there, he quoted:

Give her of the fruit of her hands, And let her own works praise her in the gates.

I was proud of him for honoring his mother. But more so me, the woman he would marry. I was worthy of his praise because I was the pure bride of his dreams. My right deeds outweighed the wrong ones. That belief motivated my mission trip to Belgium.[15] I wrote in my journal: *Richard is so much on my mind. I love to think about our marriage; being with him and knowing him better than anyone else in the world; bearing his children. Yes, those thoughts are so peaceful and lovely. I'm so happy, I want to cry.*

While in Belgium, I learned to square dance. And I played my guitar and the piano in the common room while wearing his engagement ring. We exchanged letters and cassette-tape voice messages throughout our time apart.

The next summer, I wore a white gown with puffy sleeves and said "I do" on our wedding day. We listened to both preachers in our families. My uncle and his dad quoted and preached on Ephesians 5:22, 25.

---

15   I went to Belgium through Greater Europe Mission: http://www.gemission.org/ home.

Wives, submit to your own husbands as to the Lord…. Husbands, love your wives, just as Christ also loved the church and gave himself for it.

Our vows to love, honor, and cherish would show the world a godly marriage. I was intentional to be a submissive wife and please my husband. We learned the resilience/belonging dance and didn't feel the "normal" conflict our peers experienced. "Being married is a piece of cake. It's easy," Richard told one of our friends who was going through his own marital struggles.

Some friends divorced two and three years into their marriages. But we took pride that ours worked. Our childless years seemed like an extension of fun we had in college. Even though we were college graduates, he worked in a factory and coached men's soccer at the local university. I taught piano students in our home. We lived paycheck to paycheck with enough money to pay the bills.

We had confidence to become parents since we raised our yellow Labrador puppy to be a full-grown retriever. So, we conceived. Then, forty weeks later, it was Valentine's Day.

The Tuesday night special at our local steakhouse saved us grocery money. I ate a lot of baked potato with bacon bits, butter, and shredded cheese. Not only did the sizzling prime rib make me feel heavy and miserable, but my full-term belly was more than well done.

"I'm gonna be pregnant forever," I said as we walked toward the car. "This is the time to go to the hospital. Wouldn't it be great if they had heart-shaped helium balloons waiting for me?"

"You don't feel anything?"

"Nothing. This baby's never gonna come."

"You never know." But we headed home just like other Tuesday night specials.

Throughout my pregnancy, I had checked out library books and read everything about natural births, home births, and water births. Nature could take its course, and I trusted my body to deliver a healthy child. The research showed me the best and safest birth experience for our little one and me.

Richard and I took childbirth classes. He breathed with me, and I became aware of how to focus on labor. But my new learning didn't fit the hospital system. Nor did it fit the two men who mattered: my doctor and my husband. I allowed them to overrule my insights as we prepared for a sterile and controlled hospital birth.

The rhythmic tightening started two evenings later. I agreed to ride in the wheelchair even though I could walk. The nurse insisted that I lie flat on my back rather than labor upright with gravity as my friend. She fastened a monitor and said, "Now be still. If you move, we won't be able to measure your baby's heartbeat and levels of distress."

"Okay." But I knew walking and moving would help my baby be less stressed and labor more progressive. The nurses and doctor looked at the screen and ignored me. The submission/persuasion dance made me distrust my body. I submitted to an epidural and delivered a six-and-a-half-pound baby girl who had thick, long eyelashes.

Beyond the surge of hormones, insecurities, fear, and pain, something transcended the hours of labor, tension, and the epidural. When I saw my newborn's little face and held her fragile body, a depth of love I had never known emerged. I examined her wrinkly hands and cried uncontrollably while feeling the warmth of her little body molded to mine. This love was overwhelming.

Divine love flashed through every neuron of my brain, every nerve in my body, and every fiber of my soul. I felt God holding me this close—skin to skin—as I met my little girl so helpless and new. How could I love and be loved this much?

Two years later we took another childbirth class and practiced breathing again. This time I would trust my body. Yet, after thirty hours of induced labor, my newborn came by Caesarian section.

When I looked into her small face and observed her every wrinkle, more divine love overwhelmed me like a first-time experience. Where did all this love come from? It gushed from me to my second born without subtracting from my first, nor from my husband.

Birthing her made me forget the distrust I had for the hospital system. But they took her away for observation because of hospital policy. My husband and doctor insisted. And no one noticed my tears.

The girls grew from newborns to toddlers and danced to my piano music. I hired a babysitter while reducing my student load to a part-time piano teaching business.

Our parents made yearly visits since both families lived hundreds of miles away. The church was our support system. I sang in the church choir and volunteered through teaching Sunday school.

Partnered dancing includes:
Secrecy/pretend dance
Shame/façade dance
Rejection/distance dance
Resilience/belonging dance

Richard became a full-time employee of the university with a prestigious position as sports information director. He traveled with the sports teams and received praise from athletes, coaches, interns, cheerleaders, and fans. The job provided modestly for our family of four, and our daughters needed both of us. I felt like a single mom since they rarely saw him. I knew what it was like to grow up without my dad. And I was a lonely wife. Every time I tried to tell Richard, he got angry.

"You don't understand," he said. "I love my job, and I'm good at it. I'm not working anywhere else." His opinion always overruled mine. But I had developed strong opinions since becoming a mother. My growing concern motivated me to be more diligent in my prayers. I believed my husband would have his own aha moments. He'd miss our girls. Then we'd partner as parents. He could pursue a different career and be present for his family.

Our daughters needed their dad, and I needed to be their advocate since they were so little. A letter to Richard would allow him to be reflective instead of reactive. He'd receive it when he was out of town. After I wrote it, I held the letter in prayer for two weeks. "Please, God," I prayed. "Open my husband's heart to receive this letter. Let it make a difference for the well-being of our family." Then I read it several times over to be sure it was the right thing to do.

My words were as loving and kind as my vocabulary would allow. I sealed three handwritten pages in a red envelope. Then I nestled it in his suitcase between his socks and underwear. On the outside of the envelope, I wrote, "Open only when you have time to reflect."

My message would touch those tender places in his heart. He'd listen this time.

When he called I asked, "Did you get my letter?"

"Yes."

"Did you read it?"

"Yes. We'll talk about it when I get home." He said it with impatience and irritation. But I kept praying.

Days later he came home and said, "I can't believe you wrote that letter. Here I thought it was something romantic. And you wrote this." He threw the red envelope at me in anger. My heart beat faster and I felt small again. "We already talked about this before. You don't understand. This is my dream job. What do you want me to do? Work in a factory?" He trailed off with the same persuasive dance. I submitted as I had at the hospital.

There was no other choice, just as I believed before I broke up with my high school boyfriend. But my husband wasn't my boyfriend. So

I prayed since we had agreed to the Scripture passage at our wedding ceremony. God would hear my cry. I should feel blessed. I worked hard for this marriage. I didn't deserve the good life I had. Why was I complaining? My church was there for me.

I was growing beyond my cheerleader college days and the carefree years of our childless marriage. Motherhood had transformed me, but the marriage wasn't changing. And those dances had something to do with it.

Chapter 5

AWARE OF GUILT AND SHAME

The most terrifying thing is to accept oneself completely.
—Carl Jung

Guilt is a God-given temporary emotion designed to change our moral direction. Our increased awareness shows us when we're heading in the wrong direction. Guilt's purpose is to turn us around. When we choose to do the next right thing, we no longer need that same guilt. The job is done until we become more aware of wrong. Or realize the effects of our wrong decisions.

There are two things to consider about guilt. First, chronic guilt may instead be foundational beliefs about the self. If we think we are damaged goods, we're dealing with shame instead of guilt.

Shame showed up when I failed the second grade. I thought there was something wrong with me because I couldn't read. Shame makes us believe everyone else is better than us. We don't deserve connection with the rest of humanity. We keep secret boxes in our heads so we can keep judgments out. Wrong actions are not just what we've done; they have become who we are.

Phrases such as "What's wrong with you?" or "Shame on you" permeate our cultures, school systems, politics, churches, and families. Yet these phrases are an assault on our authentic selves. They blind us to our belovedness, our worth, and our value as human beings. We then live with a small, harsh, and critical self-image.

"Shame makes us believe everyone else is better than us. We don't deserve connection with the rest of humanity. We keep secret boxes in our heads so we can keep judgments out."

Christians believe that Christ bore our shame on the cross,[16] but most don't live that way. Of course, we recognize shame as being part of human nature. If we had never struggled with shame, we'd be dangerous or psychopathic. Our task is to become shame resilient when it shows up.

The difference is this: shame is a skewed belief about the authentic self. In contrast, guilt is temporary and designed to be transformative. It helps us learn from regrets and gain wisdom toward the next right thing.

Secondly, chronic guilt could be false guilt that we've embraced as gospel truth. Other people, families, and cultures "guilt us" into their standards. The hospital system guilted me into believing I would distress my baby if I didn't labor flat on my back.

Our growing awareness helps us distinguish between guilt and shame.

---

16 Hebrews 12:2

Richard's reaction to my loving letter left me believing I had "no other choice." I continued the submission dance with the certainty of my growing faith. I put energy into being the best mother I could be for my girls even though I felt lonely and neglected. After all, my pastor's wife said that feelings didn't matter.

"Christians believe that Christ bore our shame on the cross, but most don't live that way."

One morning I woke up alone in our queen-sized bed since Richard was traveling with the team. I had been anxious and worried before, but this was different. And it was weird. It was like something I'd never experienced.

I looked around the room and felt detached, like I didn't belong in this marriage. Nor did I deserve being a mom to these two daughters. I looked down on my life as if I watched my character in a play. But I wasn't that character. It wasn't real.

All my efforts at making my marriage work, and Richard believing I was a virgin bride, were a huge lie. I had denied and repressed my past, but this seemed to come up from nowhere. The lock on the secret box in my head was just as flimsy as the metal one on my first pink-and-blue diary.

My out-of-body experience became a floodgate of heaving emotions. *What am I doing here? I have these beautiful daughters and a wonderful husband and marriage. Why am I here? My life is a lie. Richard doesn't know the real me. I don't know who I am. I can't live like this anymore. I don't belong.*

When I got up to make the girls' breakfast, my hands trembled. I cleaned up the kitchen with a lump in my throat. I tried praying and reading Scripture during their naps. But I became sick with a runny nose and cough.

While giving the youngest her bath, I couldn't hold back the floodgate of tears. I turned on the faucet so she couldn't hear my groans. She needed to stay in her two-year-old world playing with her tub toys.

A verse yelled at me from the black letters on the white pages of my blue leather Bible. *Confess your trespasses to one another… that you may be healed…*[17] I argued with God in my prayers. "I can't tell Richard this, Lord. I'd rather die. My little girls need me."

But I kept hearing God say, "Confess your trespasses…that you may be healed." The thought of telling him made me sick. But the Scripture verse wouldn't leave my head. I already memorized Psalm 103:12 and believed God had removed my sins *as far as the east is from the west…* I embedded that truth a long time ago. So why was this other verse crowding my thoughts?

The dark cloud was too much to bear alone. I called my friend Sandy, and she came over. I never trusted anyone at this level except the college girlfriend who left during the semester. But I had no other choice. I was miserable.

"Sandy, I can barely function. I've kept this secret box for a long time. It was so long ago. I forgot all about it until the other day when I woke up. I can't ignore this 'confess your faults' verse. Do you think this is God speaking to me? Or is it the world, the flesh, or the devil trying to destroy my marriage?" I referred to Christian teaching about the three enemies of our souls.[18]

"I don't know, Judy. But let me pray for you." And she prayed for wisdom and the Holy Spirit to comfort me while more tears flowed down my cheeks.

"Thank you." We embraced as soul sisters.

---

17 James 5:16
18 This teaching comes from the apostle Paul in Ephesians 2:2-3.

"I'll keep praying for you. Call me later to let me know how you're doing."

"Okay."

I felt enormous relief. Sandy was still my friend. She didn't judge or make me feel worse. She still loved me.

The dialogue continued in my head. *If I tell Richard, it will ruin us. I can't, Lord. I've worked too hard for this marriage. If I hide this struggle, we can go on like normal.* But *normal* is what I pleaded with my husband to change as I wrote in that letter with the red envelope.

When Richard came back home, it wasn't hard to conceal my grief. He was tired at the end of each day. We hadn't made flirtatious eye contact since college days. He was about to leave town for a tournament. If it didn't happen soon, it never would. Confession scenarios went through my mind. There would be a before and after. Yet I couldn't hold back. I asked him to take me out to dinner before he left the next day.

"Do you want to go parking by the river afterward?" I asked. When we were younger, we'd sneak times to be alone together and make out. On this date, it would be the time to tell him.

"Hmm…we'll see. I have a lot to pack before my trip tomorrow."

That evening we sat by the fireplace at a fine-dining restaurant. It was dark between us with a lighted candle. He didn't notice my watery eyes while I kept composure with lighthearted conversation. We ate our prime rib steak. He talked about his job, and I talked about the children. We left the restaurant as my heart kept its rapid-fire beats. As we got in the car, I wondered if he remembered my idea to go parking.

At the crucial intersection, the red light seemed to go on forever. His blinker wasn't on. The decision to go straight or turn right made the confession scenes come faster in my mind. If he went straight through the light and forgot the parking plans, I'd forget all this internal torment. I'd know it wasn't God in this anxiety that could destroy our marriage.

If he remembered, then I'd know it was a divine invitation. But it was a huge risk.

The light turned green and he made a right-hand turn toward the river park. There was no turning back. I felt blood pumping in my ears. The rippled river reflected the crescent moon. The clear, starry night and gentle breeze were eerily romantic. He parked the car, and we rolled down our windows to smell the evening. We could hear the hum of a cricket chorus.

I was about to ruin it all. This moment would change everything. Our marriage vows meant "until death do us part." But I questioned that truth. The only thing I heard through my throbbing head and nauseous stomach was "Confess your faults one to another that you may be healed."

I took a deep breath. "Richard, there's something I need to tell you." He looked at me knowing something was wrong. A long pause prefaced my words. "I…I wasn't a virgin when we got married." There. I said it. All that pretending about being a virgin bride was out in the open. I couldn't see past my tears nor the anger I imagined on his face. *Okay. He knows I wasn't his virgin bride.*

"I thought you were ready to confess an affair. Or that you hooked up with someone in Belgium." I took a deep breath of relief. *This isn't so bad.* There. I was done.

"No. That didn't happen. I've always been faithful to you."

"How did you keep from getting pregnant?"

The question dangled by a thread, and I had a choice. But I kept hearing "confess your faults…" while my breathing got shallower. I heard myself say, "I didn't. I didn't keep from getting pregnant. I had an abortion."

My body began to shake along with uncontrollable tears. I opened the car door on the verge of throwing up the prime rib. He reached over me to close the door. He put his arms around me, and my stomach settled. In his embrace, I tried making sense of what happened. But all I could feel were the arms of Jesus around my body. Through my blurry eyes, I looked up at my husband's face. I didn't see Richard. I saw Jesus.

I don't remember what either of us said after that. Richard left for his trip the next morning. But a couple of weeks went by before I could look him in the eyes without crying.

It was a supernatural beginning of deeply experiencing the forgiveness of Christ. I didn't understand it. But up until that time, it was the most sacred moment I had ever experienced. A heavy façade fell off. After nine years of marriage and two daughters, I faced the reality of an abortion.

From that point, we reflected on our history, our pictures, and our experiences. We reframed everything. I began living lighter, with appreciation and love for Richard as my husband. He became tender and nurturing toward me. Nine months later, I prepared to give birth again.

The third time around, when we barely had enough money, we hired a labor room nurse. Debbie came to the house and paid attention to me and respected my body. She breathed with me so I could labor naturally at home. She taught me how to trust my laboring body. She gave me confidence to plan and practice a natural birth after a C-section.

We went to a different hospital at the right time. I sat in a different wheelchair, and I submitted to a different doctor. And Debbie stayed with me the whole time. She didn't look at the monitors. But she watched and noticed my tears.

It was a full moon, and three other laboring women moaned in other birthing rooms. My doctor hustled from room to room. The nursing staff was busy looking at monitors. But Debbie was there instilling camaraderie between me and my doctor. She overruled my husband at times. Yet the whole time, she paid attention to me. My doctor came minutes before I birthed a little boy. Richard was there to catch him. We were a team that time.

When he held our newborn, I almost heard an audible voice from God. "Richard, this is the little boy you've always wanted. He's My gift to you. You've forgiven and loved Judy like I've forgiven and loved you." And to me, I heard God say, "Judy, this little boy is My gift to you. You took a leap of faith and confessed. You allowed Richard to love and forgive you as I have loved and forgiven you."

Beyond the surge of hormones and emotions, my faith and awareness grew. I had more than enough love as a wife, mother, and beloved daughter of God. We hadn't planned beyond our family of four. Yet neither Richard nor I could deny our marital transformation those nine months before. I could trust God whether or not He used the three-page letter in the red envelope. Heavy façades no longer covered my shame. And I was changing from the inside out.

Chapter 6

INTENTIONAL ROSE

*It is the air we breathe, and it's our vocation
to become who we are and all that we are.*
—Father Richard Rohr

Three truths have influenced my counseling practice. First, every person who contacts me or comes through my door for therapy is a divine appointment. Second, my physical office is sacred space. And, third, deep breathing helps clients become more aware. When we breathe deeply it slows our heart rate and reactions. It allows the fight/flight/freeze part of our brains (amygdala) to calm its message of danger. Temporary emotions flow rather than get stuck. Deep breaths of air open awareness to allow intentional responses.

Just as we need air to stay alive, we need AIR—a formula I use— for growth. The letters in AIR stand for awareness, intentionality, and risks. We need all three to grow into our authentic selves. All three are present in our stories of divine invitations. Awareness is first. Intentions are visions, plans, or prayers. Risks of growth only come after awareness and intentions.

For example, my letter to Richard was intentional after I became aware of my loneliness and our daughters' needs. Praying over it for two weeks also represented being intentional. The risk was giving it to him. Then I asked about it on the phone. Risks are always uncertain.

My risk didn't produce what I intended, but it moved me to another level of awareness. I risked confession of the secret box. It transformed me and changed the marital dance.

Neuroscience confirms the psychological wisdom of the ancient text of James in the Bible. My experiences made me appreciate the Catholic sacrament of confession. When we confess to one another, we break through isolation that separates us. It clears our souls from shame, anger, and resentment. It breaks through our mind's automatic harsh accusations. Confession makes us aware.

Therapy or community groups like Alcoholics Anonymous[19] or Celebrate Recovery[20] can be sacred places. They get us out of our isolation and rigid thinking. They normalize human struggles and create connections. Scripture affirms these divine invitations. *For where two or three are gathered together in My name, I am there in the midst of them.*[21]

---

19 Alcoholics Anonymous (AA), https://www.aa.org, is for those recovering from alcohol problems. Al-Anon, https://al-anon.org, is for family members to be aware of their "relationship dances" that inadvertently stagnate the messes. The same type of support with other issues includes https://saa-recovery.org and https://www.na.org.

20 Celebrate Recovery is a faith-based version of AA started in 1991 by Saddleback Church in Lake Forest, California: https://www.celebraterecovery.com. This program welcomes nonsubstance issues as well.

21 Matthew 18:20

"The letters in AIR stand for awareness, intentionality, and risks. We need all three to grow into our authentic selves. All three are present in our stories of divine invitations."

The energy of three small children filled every space in our three-bedroom rancher. Church was a place of friendships, babysitters, and social events in addition to worship. Richard was less connected since he traveled on weekends. And I felt responsible for our family's spiritual development.

We lived in a community that valued all human life. A postcard came in the mail a week before Sanctity of Life Sunday,[22] inviting us to a citywide pro-life gathering. I said to Richard, "I'm interested in this rally. Would you keep the children so I can go Saturday?"

"Sure. No problem."

A few days later, our daughters placed the plates, cups, silverware, and napkins on laminated placemats

"Awareness is first. Intentions are visions, plans, or prayers. Risks of growth come after awareness and intentions."

with diagrams while baby brother ate his appetizer of dry Cheerios from his highchair. We didn't expect their dad for supper. But he came through the door with briefcase in one hand and flowers in the other.

---

22 National Sanctity of Human Life Day was issued by President Ronald Reagan as the Sunday closest to January 22, the anniversary of Roe v. Wade. It was that day in 1973 that the Supreme Court ruled in favor of women's access to abortion: https://en.wikipedia.org/wiki/National_Sanctity_of_Human_Life_Day. It was the spring of the same year of my "procedure."

"Daddy's home!" Through my smile I thought, *How sweet! It isn't my birthday. It's not Valentine's Day. What a thoughtful husband I have!*

He held long-stemmed roses peeking out of green tissue paper. With a quick hug, I smelled them above the dinner. Then I gasped. Among the baby's breath and greenery were four roses: three red and one white. I looked at my three children around the table as I tried making sense of his loving gesture. But I felt a lump in my throat when I understood the meaning.

I stopped. The little white rose stared at me as a gentle reminder of the baby I never grieved. He was just as real as my three living children. As if I'd been asleep, the child I conceived woke me up.

At my first OB/GYN appointment I checked the box "no previous pregnancy or abortion." I delivered two daughters denying my secret box. Its lock was secure when I nursed and smelled and held my newborns close to my body.

The white rose seemed to say, "Look here. I'm with you." Then I realized I never heard him cry or watched him grow. Pain pierced my heart and tears dripped down my face. The children watched while their dad held me. I held the roses. Later that evening when the little ones were asleep, I filled a vase with water and set it on the cleared table.

Richard had arranged for the two of us to attend the pro-life gathering together. Minutes before leaving the next day, I took the white rose and left the others in their vase. Then I wrapped it with the same crinkled floral green tissue paper. "We won't be gone long," I assured the children when their sitter arrived. We hugged and kissed them goodbye. Then Richard drove us to the event where a crowd gathered. I left the rose on my seat when we got out of the car. Taking his hand, we joined the group around a platform.

Dark clouds hovered in the sky as a speaker shared a message of hope and healing. The service ended with a prayer and invitation for attendees to return to their cars and form a line. All would meet for a solemn tribute to mourn the loss of aborted babies.

My rose waited for me on the seat. With every car's headlights on, we lined up behind the other vehicles for the funeral procession to the abortion clinic. Richard and I traveled in silence with sacred respect between us while I held my tender rose.

He pulled into a parking space next to the pregnancy center. "Are you okay?" he asked.

"Yes, I'm fine." As he reached for my hand, I worried about who parked next to us. They would guess I had an abortion. What if I saw a homeschooling family or church acquaintance? I could stay in the car and reflect on my own.

He must have heard my thoughts. "We don't have to get out."

"I know." I blew my nose again. Every tissue became damp wads on the floorboard. But my rose gave me comfort. It had bloomed a little from the night before. And its fragrance permeated the car. *Maybe I can do this.* "I can't stay here. That's why I'm holding this rose. I don't care if someone sees me. I just can't stay here." I noticed the rain. The windshield wipers went back and forth. I was focused and far away, slow and fast. He turned off the engine, and the wipers stopped.

Richard opened my door and held the umbrella over me as I stepped onto the wet pavement. With head down, I left the crinkled green floral tissue and held my rose by the stem between the thorns. As we walked near, I looked up and gasped. On the sidewalk of the abortion clinic, a horizontal banner stood proudly with bold letters: *In Honor of the Babies Whose Lives Were Taken by Abortion.*

Two buckets like pillars on either side held hundreds of red roses. Mourners took them one by one and laid them on the sidewalk in front of the banner. In the silent rain, more roses were laid to rest. They must have been aborted children, grandchildren, nieces, nephews, and stepchildren. I noticed the crying faces of men, women, and children. Did they see mine? Some held each other. Others stood alone. But all were together.

I raised my little white rose to absorb its fragrance one last time. I didn't want to let it go. Kneeling close to the wet pavement, I laid it down with the others. I took a deep breath of air and whispered, "I'm sorry…"

Richard reached for me when I stood up with empty arms. I no longer slumped under the umbrella. Instead, I honored my unborn child. After moments of tears, forgiveness, and release, I said, "I'm ready now." We walked across the street to the open house at the pregnancy center.[23] The rain stopped and the clouds dispersed.

In the small, crowded lobby, a volunteer explained their services. Then she led us to the meeting room for mingling and refreshments. Through the hallway, we passed counseling rooms. The anxiety of my sixteen-year-old self showed up. But it left as quickly as it came. I wasn't that vulnerable teenager anymore. Instead, I was in my early thirties, grounded as a wife and mother.

The potent memory was no longer a threat. But the next appointment in that recollection was a walk into a brick building like this one. It was after our family doctor told my mom something like this: "Your daughter is about eight weeks pregnant. Congratulations! She's not dying of cancer. We can set her up for an appointment and start over. She can get on with her life, finish school, and go to college. She can get married at the right time and have a baby after that. She's young and has her whole life in front of her. She and you can forget all about this."

I was relieved then. But my boyfriend was Catholic, the only denomination outspoken against abortion. I judged them as wrong since I never heard pro-life messages from preachers at my church. Abortion

---

23 AAA Women's Services has been renamed to Choices Chattanooga: https://choiceschattanooga.org.

had been legalized only weeks before. But this man in a white coat was a medical doctor who knew better than two adolescents.

Mark and I knew the silence/control dance. We were also skilled in the submission/persuasion dance. I convinced him that abortion was our best option. He agreed to keep it a secret, and I promised to marry him after a semester of college.

In the waiting room at the abortion clinic, someone said, "Let's forget this day ever happened." I ignored a divine invitation after the procedure that took the life of my nine-week-old "fetus." Relief was short when I woke with a cloud of darkness just like the dark clouds on this pro-life event.

While I recovered at the facility, Mark brought me a single red rose. We grieved together. And I vowed to forget that day ever happened. We never spoke of it again.

But I walked into a pregnancy center as a grown woman. I placed my white rose next to all the red ones. I wasn't scared and pregnant. This wasn't the abortion clinic. Moms, daughters, boyfriends, and absent dads weren't avoiding human connection with others in the room. Instead, I saw compassionate faces of volunteers. Rather than sign my name to a procedure, I signed along with a list of prospective volunteers. *If only I had someone in my life then to tell me the truth…I would have given life to my baby,* I thought.

A clear divine invitation said to me, *Judy, it's time. Speak life into the hearts of frightened and confused pregnant girls. Tell them the truth.*

I joined other volunteers who learned how to counsel women with unexpected, unplanned, or unwanted pregnancies. During orientation, I found out about the post-abortion recovery program. And all volunteers who had experienced abortion were required to participate in a post-abortion Bible study. I couldn't imagine anyone admitting they've had an abortion, let alone meeting in a group!

I knew Scripture more than the average person since having participated in several Bible study groups and teaching Sunday school. Yet I was still shocked to hear of such a thing as a post-abortion Bible study. *You mean God has something to say to me through His Word about my abortion?* I had never read or studied Scripture in that context before.

Of course, I didn't need to attend a post-abortion Bible study.[24] Besides, it had been fourteen years. No one needed to know. I intended to persuade the director to allow an exception. Then I sat across from Pam.

"I'm so excited to be part of the training. I've learned so much already," I said.

"We're glad to have you, Judy," Pam said.

"I didn't realize you required volunteers to be in a post-abortion Bible study group. You see, I had an abortion as a teenager that had been a secret up until two years ago." I didn't expect another flood of tears. She handed me a box of Kleenex.

"Judy, hearing your story makes the work we do here worth it. There are some days I get so discouraged. But your story encourages me. You've already experienced a level of healing. But it will make you a more effective volunteer to participate in the group."

I was still worried about my image when I arrived on the first night of the group. A volunteer I met at training sat at the reception desk. "I'm surprised to see you here, Judy. Are you here for the Bible study?"

"Yes, I'm here to observe. I might want to volunteer in the post-abortion ministry." Denial rolled off my tongue. Then I entered a room with six other women who looked just as nervous as I felt. They had more courage than me. They weren't pretending. The leader shared her

---

24 I still have my original version of *Forgiven and Set Free* by Linda Cochrane. Although I was brave enough to write in my workbook with pencil, I wasn't ready for the permanency of ink as I was still working through my denial: http://bakerpublishinggroup.com/authors/linda-cochrane/149.

story along with clarity about the purpose and group guidelines. One by one each woman shared why she came. Then it was my turn.

"I came here tonight wanting you to believe I was a volunteer-in-training. And I am. But I also had an abortion, and I'm here for more healing."

The group was a divine invitation. I grieved and named my child. I acknowledged his humanity and short life in my womb. My aborted baby was worthy of love just as much as my three living children. The violent ignorance of my decision didn't change my mother-love for the child I tried to forget. I experienced Isaiah 49:15.

Can a woman forget her nursing child, and not have compassion on the son of her womb? Surely they may forget, yet I will not forget you.

Our ranch-style home was still small with the energy of raising three children. But my world became bigger. Richard came home early from work so I could attend my group meetings.

Chapter 7

SPEAKING AWAY SHAME

Empathy is … communicating that incredibly
healing message of, "You're not alone."
—**Brené Brown**

D
r. Brené Brown,[25] a famous professor and social scientist, sheds light on what most people avoid. Not only have her studies of courage, vulnerability, and shame gained global attention, but she's a woman after my own heart. I've experienced the truths of her research through my personal history. Her best-selling books and teachings continue to impact me in my counseling practice.

We've seen how shame is a human condition in which we need resilience. Dr. Brown clarifies that silence, secrecy, and judgment keep

---

25 I've read most of Brené Brown's books and taken CEUs (continuing education courses) from her. She offers training programs for leaders at https://brenebrown. com.

it intact.[26] To illustrate, I use a flourishing plant in my office to explain how shame grows.

I tell my clients, "A plant needs regular sunlight, water, and plant food to keep growing. Otherwise, it will shrivel up and die. If shame were a plant, it would need regular secrecy, silence, and judgment to stay alive. If it doesn't get those three things, it will eventually shrivel and lose its power over us."

Shame drives addictions like drugs, alcohol, and pornography. Shame can also drive socially acceptable behaviors like overworking or homeschooling children. Hyper-religiosity, overachievement, perfectionism, and over-responsibility can be shame-driven attitudes. Those and many other things block our authentic journey.

"Shame drives addictions like drugs, alcohol, and pornography. Shame can also drive socially acceptable behaviors like overworking or homeschooling children. Hyper-religiosity, overachievement, perfectionism, and over-responsibility can be shame-driven attitudes."

One of my spiritual directors, Father Richard Rohr, writes about scanning our thoughts for spiritual malware. When we detect "malicious software" on our computers, we need to be aware of how our minds are subject to addictive thinking.[27] Our task is to become aware of shame-driven thoughts, attitudes, and behaviors.

When our faith helps us take risks to break shame's power, we no longer bear its weight. Yet it requires daily awareness and intentionality.

---

26   Dr. Brown mentions three things that make shame grow in her 2012 Ted Talk: https://www.ted.com/talks/brene_brown_listening_to_shame#t-1137953.

27   Richard Rohr, *Just This* (Albuquerque, NM: Society for Promoting Christian, 2018), p. 111, https://store.cac.org/products/just-this.

And scanning for spiritual malware. We must first be aware then intentional before taking risks of growth.

Awareness leads us to recognize self-judgments and comparisons with others. We can be intentional to share with another person or group to weaken shame. It's risky to expose the dark places of our humanity to the light. That's when we align with our authentic selves. Again, that's why I call my counseling office sacred space. For most, it's holy ground that breaks through shame. We recognize the formula and take deep breaths of AIR: awareness, intentions, and risks.

My volunteering at the pregnancy center changed my shame dance. I risked telling my story and participated in the group. All seven of us knew each others' darkest secrets. We grieved our aborted children together.

Volunteers and staff at the center prepared for the annual fundraising banquet. The director approached me and said, "Judy, you're one of our volunteers that shines and encourages all of us here. I'm wondering if you'd be interested in sharing your testimony at the banquet. There are two other volunteers on the program. I think you'd be a positive person to represent the ministry."

"Oh, thanks. Yes. I'll do it." I felt honored and energized, but also scared.

In college I dreaded giving presentations. One professor said, "Judy, you knew your material. I'm surprised you were that nervous."

"I don't know why I get so anxious." Back then, I was still unaware of how I combined the steps of not-good-enough with the rejection dance. I didn't volunteer for "show and tell" in elementary school. From music recitals to spelling bees, I felt fear.

But the fear I avoided in the past now had a different purpose. It moved me into awareness. What could be more fear inducing than my confession to Richard? I laid down my white rose and participated in a post-abortion Bible study. When I breathed through anxiety, it opened my awareness to a larger story. Not only did I live through it, I became intentional to say yes to new opportunities. Fear became a signal toward divine invitations. But it was a risk.

Adrenaline accompanied the drive back to my stay-at-home-mom self that day. Then I remembered my college presentations. *Why did I agree to this?* I was about to tell the biggest secret of my life to a crowd of four hundred people. *Why did I say yes?*

I created an outline with an introduction, three points, and a closing on 4 x 6-inch index cards. I practiced in front of the mirror and recorded my voice on the portable cassette player. Multiple recordings and playbacks minimized my "ums" and "so's." I practiced until I could do it in my sleep. Nervousness turned into energy.

Our trusty babysitter came as Richard and I kissed the children goodbye for the evening. Crystal chandeliers hung from beams of the cathedral ceiling. Floral candlelit centerpieces with china place settings adorned a room full of white linen-covered round tables. After a few handshakes and smiles, a volunteer led us to our table near the front of the stage. Before I sat down, I walked to the podium to calm my nerves.

> "When our faith helps us take risks to break shame's power, we no longer bear its weight. Yet it requires daily awareness and intentionality... We must first be **aware** then **intentional** before taking **risks** of growth."

The room quickly filled with people dressed in semi-formal attire. I walked back to our table and sat with others we had never met before. The poise and kindness of the servers made me feel like British royalty.

The master of ceremonies welcomed guests, and a clergy person prayed for the meal. They stood behind the same podium that I would stand behind later in the program. I became aware of every detail that happened on that stage. Live piano music accompanied the chatter of guests. My stomach was too nervous to eat much. I imagined the taste of cheesecake topped with chocolate and strawberries. Maybe I could eat it after my speech.

The program began, and I couldn't stop it. I was the last volunteer up. The first woman walked to the stage. She described her pregnant and scared self from three years before. Her husband joined her holding their two-year-old son. I felt small comparing my story with hers. She was courageous. I wasn't.

The other volunteer stood proudly between two older adolescent females. She was their mentor. One girl was very pregnant. The other was a mom of a newborn. This volunteer's story was full of life. Mine wasn't. Those women were unlike me. They walked off the stage, and everyone applauded.

I was next and felt the same anxiety as when Richard turned right at the stoplight. Everything would change. There would now be a before and after. I wasn't worried about all four hundred of those people. Some were volunteers who knew and accepted me. But the people from my church would see me differently. My heart beat faster. I couldn't do the secrecy/pretend dance anymore. I felt the rhythm of rejection.

I had no other choice but to get out of my seat and walk to the stage. I took my place behind the podium. I had no story of giving life to my baby, but I had my 4 x 6-inch index cards in my hand with my three-point outline.

I wasn't in front of the dresser mirror or talking into my cassette player. The bright lights made it impossible for me to see a crowd of judgmental faces. The room was quiet. They waited. Did they hear my heartbeat? I spoke into the microphone.

"I want to tell you about a young woman whose life was deeply touched by this ministry." The only way I could prepare this speech was to speak in the third person. I talked about a "young woman" as if she were a client I helped.

"This young woman became pregnant at sixteen. Her doctor and others said she could start all over. The procedure was as simple as a tooth extraction. It was safer to have an abortion than to have a baby. They said she had her whole life ahead of her. She could have the procedure, never to think of it again. She felt relief."

My mouth felt like cotton, and I could only speak after a long pause. "I was that sixteen-year-old girl." I was sure I heard their gasps. My tongue stuck to the roof of my mouth before I took another long breath and told them the story of my confession to Richard. "I broke free from the secret and had a little boy nine months later. Then I left my little white rose behind and entered the front doors of the pregnancy center. My volunteering there changed my life.

"I had already experienced a level of forgiveness. But then I joined the post-abortion Bible study. I met with six other ladies. We all learned to grieve together. And although he was in my womb a short time, I named him Courtney. And I don't know why, but that name kept coming to me because I didn't know whether he was a boy or a girl. The name could be either. And it just felt right to name him that.

"Then I read Psalm 100 verse 4: *'Enter into His gates with thanksgiving, and into His courts with praise.'* Courtney's name means one who lives at court. I know that I'll join him one day in heaven. That gives me peace to make a difference now.

"He is just as real as my living children, and I honor his dignity and worth as a human being. One who lived a short time in my womb but transformed me this many years later."

I ended my talk with closing words from a letter I wrote to Courtney in my grief. "I imagine you in heaven being with your granddad. Maybe you have gotten to know him well, and you have a special relationship.

Your granddad may have told you all about when I was a little girl. I love you, son. I'll see you soon. Love, Mom."

The lights were still bright, and I couldn't see anyone's face. My nervousness turned to calm, and I looked down so I wouldn't trip as I walked off the stage. I found my seat next to Richard at our table. He put his arm around me and whispered, "You did a good job." Tempted to avoid eye contact, I raised my head to the other eight people we met over small talk. Now they knew. But I saw empathy and trust in their eyes. They weren't the judgmental faces I had imagined.

This same crowd who applauded for the other volunteers clapped for me. Everyone stood up. But I sat there with my untouched strawberry and chocolate cheesecake.

As the program ended, I stood. Several approached me and shook my hand. There was a line waiting. One by one, we made eye contact. Some were teary. Others gave gentle hugs and whispers. "That happened to me too."

I received other speaking invitations. The next one was at my church. And I was even more nervous. Church people knew me, unlike others. They knew I was a fourth-grade Sunday school teacher and sang alto in the choir. They knew my children, and I knew theirs. They knew Richard.

As I said yes to opportunities, I still struggled with the dance of secrecy. I could walk up to a podium and speak with confidence. But right after getting off the stage, I began the familiar dance of shame again. Yet the more I did it, the weaker that dance became.

Chapter 8

INTENTIONAL TRANSITIONS

To exist is to change, to change is to mature,
to mature is to go on creating oneself endlessly.
—Henri Bergson

A growing marriage requires two individuals learning to be aware and intentional. Moving through and beyond conflict can lead to connection. Lifelong intimate relationships can help us develop empathy that wouldn't happen otherwise. With awareness each can be intentional to join hands with God and become each other's soul healers. Trust and vulnerability require intentional partnership.

Another of my mentors, Dr. John Gottman,[28] is world renowned for his research on marital stability. His findings are packaged in books for the general public and clinical training programs for therapists like

---

28 I received clinical trainings from Drs. John and Julie Gottman, whose teachings have made a huge impact in my work with couples.

me. He helps us understand differences between "the masters" and "the disasters." In other words, those who grow beyond their marital messes are the "masters." Those who get stuck are the "disasters." Certain behaviors and attitudes put us heading in one direction or the other.

Gottman challenges our previously held beliefs about how therapists help or hinder the couples they work with. For example, we shouldn't focus solely on conflict resolution skills. The reason is that 69 percent of conflict in our relationships is perpetual. It has no resolve. But there are invitations for growth.

"A growing marriage requires two individuals learning to be aware and intentional. Moving through and beyond conflict can lead to connection. Lifelong intimate relationships can help us develop empathy that wouldn't happen otherwise."

If you divorce one spouse and marry another, you can be assured of a different set of perpetual conflicts. They're likely to add up to the same 69 percent as the old marriage. The wisdom here is for couples to learn how to solve the 31 percent of conflicts that are resolvable. Then learn to grow through, adapt, and even appreciate the remaining perpetual 69 percent—unless, of course, part of that 69 percent dishonors the dignity, value, and worth of either spouse. Those who are open and willing to respect differences are among the "masters." Those who allow bitterness, resentment, and negativity are among the "disasters."

Speaking engagements drew women to groups I facilitated. The women in my groups gave me a more intimate view than speaking to large crowds. I became known as the "abortion lady" at church. Some avoided eye contact when I dropped off my children at the nursery. But I wasn't offended because I understood their fear. My freedom from shame helped bring healing to others. The jealousy I used to have of other women seemed to disappear.

> "With awareness each can be intentional to join hands with God and become each other's soul healers. Trust and vulnerability require intentional partnership."

One of my friends said to me, "Judy, I'd like to go through your group, but I can't."

"Why? Is it your schedule?"

"No, not that. I'm afraid my mom would find out. I tell her everything. But I couldn't tell her this."

"Oh. I'm here in case you change your mind."

Then a few weeks later my friend's mom approached me and said, "Judy, I'm proud of you for what you're doing here. I've never told anybody this, but I had an abortion before my daughter was born. It would crush her if she knew about it. If it weren't for that, I'd be the first to sign up for your group."

"Oh. It may be healing for her to know that."

"Oh, no. I'd never tell her. It was so long ago. And I don't need the group now." I knew what it was like to believe you didn't need it. I wondered if they ever would tell the other since they shared the same family secret. Would that kind of mother/daughter openness break cycles of shame? I became aware of generational patterns. If grandparents or parents struggled in the same way, it sure wouldn't feel so isolating.

I also became more aware of how others' healing journeys differed from mine. Abortion recovery doesn't come in a neat little package with a bow to unwrap. For many, abortions are consequences of incest, rape, or adultery. The effects of drug and alcohol addictions, eating disorders, and sexual promiscuity make those clouds of denial even darker.

My story seemed simple compared to the collective traumas and stories of others. Beyond the fear, helplessness, and horror, my awareness increased as I saw visual evidence of freedom. For some, even their physical postures changed in those weeks we met together. Shoulders no longer slumped. Instead of bowed heads, they made eye contact with each other. They listened and wept together. The trust was tangible. They shared their experiences for the first time. Their human dignity and worth showed on their faces. Some found their calling and signed up for training to become leaders. Deep friendships and connections continued beyond the group. The authentic power of trusting relationships broke through the darkness of secrecy.

It didn't take long for local mental health professionals to know about the group. Many licensed counselors, psychiatrists, and psychologists started referring their clients and patients. Each group had its own personality. I learned of deep soul wounds and traumatic experiences of others. For many, abortion recovery was the catalyst for transformation.

A new thought took shape: I considered training to become a counselor. But I was too busy raising three small children.

A few weeks after speaking at a women's event, I was a week late getting my period. "There's no way I can be pregnant," I said to Richard.

"It's unlikely. Let's not worry about it. You've been late before."

"Yeah, you're right. It might be the stress of speaking. Or my groups."

"Yeah, Judy. You need to slow down."

"I know."

My friend and I watched each other's children every other week. One day during my three-hour shift at the pregnancy center, I confided in my volunteer friend Sally, "Do you think it's normal for me to miss my period with all these changes I'm going through?"

"Well, Judy, you know you're in the best place to find out. We have plenty of pregnancy tests for clients here. Why don't you just take one yourself? Here." And she handed me a kit and pulled out a pair of surgical gloves from the supply box.

"Thanks," I said. "I might as well." We were slow that day. I took the gloves and kit to the bathroom. This would relieve Richard and me of uncertainty.

I squeezed a drop of urine on the strip and waited. After a few minutes, I saw a faded plus sign. Oh my gosh. I walked out of the bathroom and showed Sally. "Do you think this is a plus sign?"

"Hmm. It's pretty faded, but it looks like it to me." She looked at me and smiled.

"I can't believe it. Please, don't say anything. You're the first to know. I've got to think of a way to tell Richard."

We hadn't planned for this. Richard was overloaded with stress from work. Here I was helping other women face their unplanned pregnancies. Why was I starting to feel just as scared? He still traveled out of town. We still lived paycheck to paycheck. We'd need to sell our house and find a bigger one to raise our four children. We barely had enough money, time, and partnership. How would we do it for a family of six?

We were okay as long as we didn't talk through our differences. Even after those divine invitations in the car and his giving me roses, I noticed his growing resentment. Waves of moodiness became more frequent. Sometimes he opened up. That's when I believed my prayers, fasting, and compassion helped.

"Richard, you know that bitterness is cancerous to our marriage."

"I know."

"Don't you think it's time to let go? Our children need you, and I need you. We can't deny how God has transformed us."

"I know."

At times he listened. He'd go to church with us and be tender with me. But it took my persuasion dance. And I kept journaling my prayers when anxiety, fear, or loneliness overwhelmed me.

It took a lot of persuasion for Richard to attend marriage enrichment weekends. We came back each time feeling more connected. But it was a matter of weeks before he withdrew again. I no longer did the silence/submission dance. We became less synchronized. I hoped this "unplanned" baby would make a difference. I wondered if that was how God would soften his heart.

My teaching piano decreased to part-time with each baby's birth. We agreed for me to be a stay-at-home mom. I believed in a higher purpose of raising human beings. These little children would grow to become husbands and wives, and moms and dads. Our lifestyle was less than a two-parent income. But neither of us was materialistic.

Our limited income eliminated the possibility of private school. I persuaded Richard that homeschooling was the best option for our children. Besides, our large church had an upscale library and children's programs. There were homeschooling groups with organized PE, music, art, and sign language classes.

He agreed. But Richard and I became gridlocked in our values about how to spend and save money. Like the "disasters," we couldn't talk about it. My prayers and growing faith gave me hope that he would experience his own divine invitations. It had happened before with his tender embrace and surprise roses.

Throughout months of pregnancy, the contrast between distance and togetherness continued its waves. Richard's irritability came from nowhere. And I became aware of my critical attitude.

I had renewed hope with each child's birth. We would enter into a deeper stage of togetherness. God and Richard would come through. They'd provide for the emotional, spiritual, and financial needs of our family. He was the loving dad I didn't have as a child.

My fourth baby came naturally as a nine-pound, ten-ounce boy. And like the other three, this birthing experience ranked among the happiest days of my life. It brought that surge of love as if it were a first-time experience again. This time three siblings (eight, six, and three) hovered around our newborn, and I sensed the deep feelings of connection as a family. Our love kept multiplying.

I didn't have time to lead post-abortion Bible studies anymore. But I continued occasional public speaking. It seemed like more than a coincidence that our son's birth happened on the anniversary of legalized abortion in our country as I tried balancing motherhood with speaking. I had a broader purpose. Yet for now I was busy raising four children.

Each of my newborn's transition from the womb to the outside world made me feel like I was being born again. I became aware of the bigger world outside myself. Each child changed my status and enveloped every ounce of my womanhood.

I had become a mother of one, then two, then three, then four. One by one, each child became a sibling to the others. Where did all this love come from? Being a mother touched a deep place in my soul like no other. Years later, my spiritual director, Dr. David G. Benner,[29] said, "Judy, you really are a mother at your core, aren't you?"

"Yes," I said.

My authentic self emerged through birthing babies and mothering them well. My four children were part of God's restoration from my foolish decision at the age of sixteen. Contribution through ministry was another part of that. Motherhood is a deep place in the heart of a woman. All who've birthed, or experienced stillbirth, miscarriage, or abortion, know this deeply. But sometimes insecurities, grief, shame, self-judgment, and chronic guilt cloud that reality.

---

29   There's more about Dr. Benner in the following chapters: https://www. drdavidgbenner.ca/professional-life/.

Chapter 9

INTENTIONAL VALUES

With everything that has happened to you, you can either
feel sorry for yourself or treat what has happened as a gift.
—Wayne W. Dyer

ouples who come for therapy learn how to reverse destructive
attitudes that Dr. Gottman calls the Four Horsemen.[30] Based
on metaphorical language from the book of Revelation, these
horsemen trot into marriages creating the apocalypse of doom. Each of
the four has distinct and observable characteristics.

---

30   Many of Gottman's books reference the Four Horsemen. Among them are: John
J. Gottman, PhD, and Nan Silver, *The Seven Principles for Making Marriage
Work* (New York: Three Rivers Press, 1999), and John M. Gottman, PhD, Julie
Schwartz Gottman, PhD, and Joan DeClaire, *10 Lessons to Transform Your
Marriage* (New York: Three Rivers Press, 2006), https://www.gottman.com/
professionals/products.

The first horseman is Criticism, which is more damaging than normal complaints. Rather, it attacks the spouse's character. These criticisms usually come in "you" statements with negative traits attached. Examples are:

- "You didn't make me coffee this morning. You don't love me."
- "You didn't make the bed. How could you be so lazy?"
- "I can't believe you. No one in their right mind would…"

The next horseman is Defensiveness. This one shifts blame rather than taking responsibility using if-then statements.

- "If you wouldn't (fill in the blank), then I wouldn't (blank)."
- "You drank more than me last night. I wouldn't have gotten drunk if you hadn't opened that bottle of wine."
- "You made me mad. If you hadn't provoked me, I wouldn't have done that."

Four Horsemen
Criticism
Defensiveness
Contempt
Stonewalling

The next horseman, Contempt, includes name-calling, sneering, mockery, and hostile humor. This one is even deadlier than the first two since it feeds from long-term negative thoughts about the other. Eye rolls, sarcasm, and cynicism are symptoms of this horseman.

The last horseman is Stonewalling. That's when a partner ignores his spouse. He looks away when she speaks. He acts as if she's invisible. Of course, this angers her more as she tries to connect. But instead, it's like talking to a stone wall.

Men who are stonewalled by their wives have less physiological distress than women who are stonewalled by their husbands. Females experience increased heart rate and blood pressure. Panic attacks and anxiety are more prevalent among women "stonewallees."

We sold our three-bedroom rancher and bought a four-bedroom split foyer. The fenced backyard, kid-friendly neighborhood, and cul-de-sac were perfect for raising our children. It was springtime, when pink azalea bushes were in full bloom along with dogwood trees. An imported banana magnolia overarched the stone walkway. This was a new beginning. Our screened-in back porch with storm windows served as an ideal homeschooling room. In the mornings when it was peaceful, it became sacred space in which to read Scripture and journal my prayers.

When it came to raising our daughters, I felt my innate feminine intuition take over. But I needed insight into my little sons. So reading John Eldredge's book *Wild at Heart*[31] helped me value the adventures and risks necessary for a man-child's development. I was aware of how my strong personality could overprotect our sons. And I didn't want to plant seeds of insecurity. Rather, I wanted my boys' confidence to align with their masculine hearts. I didn't know their dad's heart very well.

We agreed to homeschool the children through early grades. But I hoped Richard would realize how valuable it was for them. Then he'd agree to continue into higher grades. Instead, he was bothered by my doing too much. And no matter how hard I tried, I struggled to be organized. My overcommitted schedule was filled with extracurricular activities and field trips. He wanted the children to play school sports and valued their socializing beyond the homeschooling and church groups. And I hadn't yet been diagnosed or treated for ADD.

----

31 John Eldredge, *Wild at Heart: Discovering the Secret of a Man's Soul* (Nashville: Thomas Nelson, 2011). For more understanding about my daughters, I later read *Captivating: Unveiling the Mystery of a Woman's Soul* (Nashville: Thomas Nelson, 2010), written by the husband/wife team, John and Staci Eldredge.

Finances, parenting, education, and spiritual training became gridlocked issues. I surrendered my homeschooling values hoping it would be one less insecurity for our children. It was becoming their "normal" to experience the Four Horsemen between me and their dad.

One day we raised our voices in a verbal fight more than usual. Our six-year-old son ran to his room. We stopped and looked at each other. I went to his room and saw him lying facedown on his bed.

"Oh, Steven. What's the matter, my son?" I asked while I rubbed his back. He turned around and sat up. His dad sat on the other side.

With quivering lips and anguished face, he said, "Are you going to get a divorce?"

At the same time, Richard and I both said, "No, of course not."

"Why do you think that?" his dad asked.

"Because it sounds like it. Jimmy's parents got a divorce, and I'm afraid you will too."

"Oh, I'm so sorry." We were still in unison.

"We shouldn't fight like that," I said.

"We promise you, we'll never get divorced. Sometimes we fight. But it doesn't mean we'll get a divorce. You can be assured of that," Richard said. And I wholeheartedly agreed.

We dried his tears and believed our promise. Thankful to have this level of partnership, I hoped our marriage would change. But the horsemen remained.

We enrolled all four children in recreational sports. They played soccer, softball, and baseball. Richard believed team sports would teach them life lessons they couldn't get otherwise. Their developing skill sets as players would land them college scholarships.

"My dad never came to any of my soccer games," he told me one day. "He was too busy as a pastor and didn't have time for me. Our kids will know that I care. I won't miss any of their games."

Steven played in a baseball tournament with his dad as head coach. He was at bat with two outs in the final inning. Bases were loaded. He had hit homers before and needed a triple to be the team's hero and win.

Parents cheered and yelled in the stands. The opposing team's chatter in the dugout sounded like this.

"Heyyyyy… batta, batta… heyyyy, batta, batta… SWING!" He swung the metal bat and missed it by a ping.

"STEEEEE…RIKE," declared the umpire with his full-body hand motion.

"Shake it off, Steven. You've got it. You can do it, buddy," the other coach said. There's an agreement among coaches to coach each other's sons to avoid undue father/son pressure.

Steven stepped away from the plate with several mock swings in the air. Back into position, he oozed confidence.

"Heyyyyy… heyyyy… batta, batta, batta." A long dramatic pause ensued before the pitcher threw the next ball. "Heyyy…" The ball passed across home plate. Steven stood tall with a pivot back off the base. All who saw claimed it was a ball. But the umpire called it otherwise.

"STEEEEE…RIKE TWO." Again, with his full-body hand motion. It seemed the guy took pleasure in such drama.

"Stay cool, Steven." With a pat on his butt, the coach said, "You've got it this time. Don't let them pressure you. You can do it." Then with a few more mock swings, Steven stepped back up to the plate.

"Heyyyy… batta, batta, batta…" The opposing team tried to distract him. But he kept his head in the game. Another ball went directly over the plate. He hit it full and hard. The shortstop player caught the grounded ball and threw it smack into the first-base player's glove. With full force, Steven's body stretched in a cloud of dust as he hit the ground. His arms reached the base. But the front slide was milliseconds too late.

The winning team, parents, and coaches jumped up and down with hugs and cheers. Steven got up, yanked his helmet off, and threw it down in anger. Other dads consoled their sons. But Richard had fire in his eyes as he pointed his finger in Steven's face. His mean stare and harsh voice said something like this.

"YOU STOP THAT. Pick up that helmet, and don't you ever do that again."

Steven stooped to pick up his helmet with one hand and threw his bat in defiance with the other. I noticed his tears; Richard didn't. Both man-child and man were angry, but Steven was a little boy. His dad was a grown man.

"What's wrong with you? That's pitiful. You pick up that bat and come over here." Richard's critical words embodied the first horseman.

His harshness toward our son was NOT the message John Eldredge wrote in his book. This crossed a boundary before I knew what verbal abuse was. My conscience didn't allow me to be silent. I stood up.

As discreetly as I could, I said, "Richard, let it go. He's only nine. The other dads and coaches aren't treating their sons like this."

He glared at me. "Leave us alone. They don't care like I do. You don't understand."

"I do understand. And I won't leave you alone," I said.

Others saw Steven's tears and quivering lips. I wasn't about to subject my son to his dad's mistreatment. This was NOT overprotection of a mom who didn't understand her son's masculine heart. I listened to my own heart this time. Richard needed me to intervene given his chronic stress and negativity. He wasn't thinking clearly through the adrenaline rush. But I couldn't convince him of that on the ball field or at home.

"Come on. Let's go," I said. Steven hesitated as he looked at me, then at his dad. He didn't know who to ride home with that night.

The tournament experience was more than two rival teams. It was more than a harsh scolding from the head coach to a vulnerable nine-year-old player. It was an extension of the contempt in our family. We left the ball field and came home as we'd done many times before. Richard remained the head coach, and I was his opponent. We fought over the players, our children. Negativity and confrontation were the playing fields in our split-foyer home. But all of us became losers. My husband stonewalled me there, yet he came alive with energy on the baseball fields.

I saw the consequences but felt helpless. It had been years since Richard chose his dream career over my loving handwritten letter in the red envelope. And I wrote letters in my prayer journals in the sacred space of the back porch.

Chapter 10

INTENTIONAL EDUCATION

Security is mostly a superstition.
Life is either a daring adventure or nothing.
—Helen Keller

When a couple comes in for counseling, their relationship is my client. Even though they are two individuals, the focus is on the well-being of their marriage. In some cases, couples counseling is not appropriate. For example, is drug or alcohol abuse an ongoing issue? Is there a sexual or emotional affair going on? Is either spouse a victim of situational or characterological domestic violence? And a more difficult issue to assess is emotional or verbal abuse. In other words, the well-being of each spouse must be honored through couples work. If it can't, it's time for individual therapy.

Many relationship therapists can be fooled by the most clever and charming of spouses who abuse. I don't like labeling individuals as "abusers" or any other derogatory term. Therapists can inadvertently harm the bullied spouse if they lack additional training. The power/control dances of emotional abuse are ingrained in our society. It's vital for therapists to have acute self-awareness. They hold power in the counseling office that can repeat what victims experience at home. Too many in our field have unknowingly caused harm by a lack of awareness.

"When a couple comes in for counseling, their relationship is my client. Even though they are two individuals, the focus is on the well-being of their marriage."

I'm not suggesting that we perceive one partner in a marriage as the victim and the other as the villain. But we must recognize that couples counseling could cause more harm than good. Both must be willing and teachable to overcome the power/control dance. If not, individual counseling for each can help them gain a sense of clarity for necessary change.

Subtle resentments crept up in me at the ball fields while buying corndogs at the concessions. We missed meals around the dinner table and were isolated from positive influences of extended family. The other players' families took time out for vacations. But Richard wouldn't allow it. He was religious about games and practices. Team sports trumped everything. It didn't matter that we couldn't afford tournament fees, uniforms, and trophies.

I learned how to cope by carrying a book with me to every game and ball practice. "Mom, you missed that double I just hit!" Then I'd look up and pay attention. But living my life sitting in bleachers wasn't how I wanted to create memories for our family.

Richard's "dream career" gradually ended. Administration changes seemed just as difficult as our marital shifts. He was the victim of unfair treatment. Low motivation, hours of watching TV, and unemployment stretched into months of detachment. He didn't follow through with men from church who initiated friendships and job opportunities. There were times our Sunday school class provided meals. We received anonymous gifts of money to pay the mortgage. He borrowed our friends' vintage truck. To make matters worse, we had a flooded basement and overflowing septic tank. It had been months since the last paycheck from earned income.

My hair turned premature gray, and I wore discouragement on my face. He never wanted me to color it, and I never bought clothes for myself. Consumer debt increased. I couldn't rely on Richard's financial provision, so I researched grants and student loans to invest in a degree program to become a counselor. In one of my prayer journal entries I wrote:

Dear Lord, in my spirit, You've told me it's not me or the children that's setting off his irritability and moodiness… I choose to see the big picture when just a small part looks so ugly.

Richard settled into a supercenter retail job with half the income of his university career. We couldn't talk about decreasing expenses. Within his first month at the new job, he bought a new truck. He returned our friends' old treasured vehicle along with a year's worth of mileage.

Our family spent hours at the ball fields. I sat on the metal bleachers, hyper-focused with my head in a textbook and a highlighter in my hand. Churning in the background of my mind was how my dad's cancer left my mom a widow. She had three children to raise. It was sudden. But my marriage was dying a slow death. Abandonment was too familiar. Unlike my mom, I had time to prepare. I was responsible for four human beings.

"HEADS UP," a parent shouted to get my attention. I jumped when a ball pinged a row up from my seat. I tried acting cool even though I was startled.

"Thanks. I need to move anyway."

———————

I enrolled in the smallest degree program to qualify for a counseling position at a church or nonprofit. When I realized the marriage enrichment weekends didn't help, we went to couples counseling with several different therapists.

"They never work," he said.

"Our counselor can't do the work for us."

And our last one said, "I suggest you both see individual therapists. Marriage counseling is not appropriate for you two at this point." My efforts didn't matter. We couldn't partner. Resistance, unemployment, and stressful incidences kept us stuck in our mess.

I didn't want to face the deadly wounds, but I couldn't let go of my hope for Richard to be the husband God designed him to be. Our children's well-being was at stake.

Our home was like the relationship. When something broke, it never got fixed. Internal rage became graffiti inside closet doors. Fist-sized holes in the walls were evidence of outward fury. No one was getting a sports scholarship. No money was saved for college.

Penny, my counselor, told me, "Judy, you've tried being both mom and dad. It's simply not possible." She waited in silence as my tears welled up. "I know this is hard to hear, but you'll need to face your loss." Another long pause closed in on me. "It's important for you to grieve."

"I know. I've known for a long time." She waited while I faced that reality. I'd need to let go of prayerful pleading and expectations. My relationship with Christ was driven by perpetual desperation.

Both superficial and close friends at church had known me for years. Some admired my martyrdom. It was a godly thing for a quiet and submissive wife to endure a difficult marriage. I trusted Scripture and interpretations from the pulpit of 1 Corinthians 7:16.

For how do you know, O wife, whether you will save your husband?

Some came to me for spiritual advice or relationship help. Others thought I was a single mom. They watched my children grow from the nursery to the youth group. But my family was falling apart. I couldn't fit them into the theological box of my faith.

I earned a two-year master's degree in five years. And I heard many "heads ups."

When all the children went to "regular school," I got two part-time jobs. One was at the pregnancy center and the other was working as a counselor in an industrial plant. With both positions (one working with mostly female clients and the other with mostly males), I discovered a "professional" part of myself. Along with filling the gaps financially, I felt heard and respected. My family wouldn't listen, but my influencing others happened effortlessly in these environments. I empathized more with women than men in troubled marriages like mine. I hoped Richard would get out of his funk. Maybe I could win his love and attention if he saw me as a professional woman.

Initials by my name and lack of management training made my title as abortion recovery director bigger than my paycheck. My strong personality could offend other staff and volunteers at both settings without my awareness. My submission dance changed into a bold/confrontation dance. Something rose up in me when I discerned mistreatment, lies, or others being wronged.

One morning I called my therapist, asking if she had any last-minute cancellations. I couldn't sleep the night before and had shortness of breath. My hands shook as I packed the children's school lunches. When I dropped off my son from the car-rider line, he asked, "Are you all right, Mom?"

"I'm not feeling well this morning. But I'll be fine after a little rest. I love you." I gave him a hug before he got out of the car.

"Love you too."

When I knew he couldn't see me, I burst into tears. I freshened up at the house and drove to my appointment. Penny knew the backstory of my counseling blue-collar workers and their families. I presented workshops and helped resolve conflicts among employees at the plant. They came to my office for encouragement, advice, and counsel. Each week the small group of volunteers and staff at this nonprofit met for breakfast. They were my tribe. Some became trusted girlfriends who knew the heartache of my marriage.

When I settled on Penny's couch, details poured out of my discovering the boss had tapped my business phone. "For two years he listened in on every conversation I had with clients and coworkers." Anger spilled from my voice. "And I trusted this man!" She listened as I shared more. "Oh my gosh. Now that I'm telling you this, I remember other hints of deception with him. How could I be so blind?"

"Judy, be easy on yourself. Men like this can be convincing." She mentioned another situation with a male authority I had brought up in counseling. Some were leaders who lacked empathy and thrived on admiration. "I'm going to ask you a question that you might not need to answer right now." She paused a moment. "Are you aware of the little-girl self who still misses the dad who left her?"

"I don't know."

"I wonder if that's why you're drawn to strong male authorities with control issues."

My emotional turmoil made sense as I walked out of her office. It wasn't just me. And maybe it wasn't me at all. I took deep breaths as I let her question sink into my soul. This incident with my boss had deeper meaning for my awareness. I became intentional about what I couldn't ignore. It was a risk, and my marriage was still falling apart.

My boss responded to my confrontation. "The phone belongs to the business, Judy. Now I realize I could have told you that I accessed your conversations. But I didn't do anything wrong." I didn't buy into his reasoning, and he fired me on the spot. "I'll hire a crew to get your furniture out of the office by Monday."

"What?"

"You can't trust me, and you need to leave immediately."

"What about my caseload? Don't you know this is unethical? These clients trust me."

"This is my decision, and I'll explain to the owner. I'll give you a severance for the next couple months. You should be thankful for that."

Nothing I said mattered. My integrity was in question by my tribe, my clients, and the plant owner. It was time I removed my association from this leader and his nonprofit organization.

A few more counseling sessions with Penny helped settle my body. My mind was still scattered. But I slept better with my authentic self intact.

Chapter 11

INTENTIONAL DEVELOPMENT

Never let the odds keep you from doing what
you know in your heart you were meant to do.
—H. Jackson Brown Jr.

O ur friends who've been married more than forty years tell me they've had several different marriages and spouses. "We're not that same new bride and groom when we said, 'I do.'"

All stages of marriage open dimensions of our journey that we couldn't imagine before. And each transition moves us into a "different" marriage. Most of us begin with a lustful romance. Through building careers and having children, we settle into an ebb and flow of adjustments. Each juncture is a choice to become aware and intentional. We can be mindful of our formula by breathing in fresh AIR: awareness, intentions, and risks.

Scary choices are necessary risks for growing wisdom. Although we can never know for certain when we encounter a divine invitation, we can choose to live by faith.

Our challenge is to risk vulnerability and intimacy with ourselves and our spouse. It's common to be misaligned when one spouse grows while the other doesn't. But changes are inevitable. And we need to grow beyond messy relationships and marriages.

We can't make another person think, feel, behave, or grow the way we think they should. It's normal in childhood to make-believe with pretend people, whether they're stuffed animals, Barbies, or GI Joes. But those who don't grow in awareness will take their pretend-people mentality into their adult relationships. This creates not only messy relationships, but it also assaults the other person.

Here are questions to ponder as we examine the pictures of our souls.

- Do you feel more loved than you did a year ago?
- What poor habits have you conquered over the last ten years?
- What reference points have changed the direction of your life?
- What is important to you now that was insignificant five years ago?
- What are you aware of now that you used to be clueless about?
- How is your picture of God (or yourself) different from what it was years ago?

Rather than learning how to honor another real human being with differences, they stay in their childish fantasies. Those who don't grow up and become more aware cheapen both theirs and others' dignity, value, and worth. We're not toys to be manipulated or controlled. The power/control dance is at the hub of any kind of abuse.[32] Getting beyond messy relationships require adults to grow out of their childish ways of being.

We can see how our younger selves have grown by looking at photos from years past. Growing thoughts and beliefs are not as evident, however.

Of course, time periods and spiritual difference can vary with questions on page 83. The idea is to be aware of our growth and how we believe, think, and behave differently from previous times.

If we're in our mid-fifties and still think like a twenty-year-old, it's time to become aware. We're designed to grow in wisdom throughout our lives. Our closest relationships invite us into our authentic journey. Every stage expands our roles and exposes our issues. As we accept the phases of our lives, we can appreciate the growing dimensions of our spouses. But it takes a lifetime practice of grace, love, and forgiveness. It's possible to grow into the bigger story of our integrity and learn self-compassion. For marriage, it takes two who are willing.

"Our challenge is to risk vulnerability and intimacy with ourselves and our spouse."

---

32 The National Domestic Violence hotline website shows the power/control wheel: https://www.thehotline.org/is-this-abuse/abuse-defined/.

I sat in the sacred space of Penny's office listening to the soft music that made my heart open. I needed her guidance, not just her comfort.

"Judy," she said, "I strongly believe you need to move forward with becoming licensed. I can imagine you in private practice. You have what it takes."

"Really?"

"Yes. Don't let the experiences of those two years discourage you. Being a counselor is your calling. I think you know that."

"I do. But I thought it was too late. It'll take another two years of classes. And two more of supervision. I'm too old to start now."

"Won't you be the same age after four years anyway?"

"Well, yeah."

"Would you rather be four years older with or without being a licensed counselor?"

"I see what you mean. I hadn't thought of it that way." As I left her office, I couldn't wait to gather my transcripts and syllabi.

I sat across the desk from Dr. Carson, the school dean who became my advisor. I told him about counseling in the nonprofit ministry. He looked at my transcripts, and I imagined him shaking his head with an "I'm so sorry we can't help."

"Judy, Tennessee is one of the strictest states for licensure. You'd qualify for a student loan if you earned another degree rather than just adding classes."

"Oh! I didn't expect that."

"You'll need to fill out the application right away. Classes start in two weeks."

I left his office excited. But I doubted. Not only was this a risk, but it was also a huge investment of time and energy. Penny was right. I couldn't be both mom and dad. I also couldn't add another thing to my scattered life. What could I let go of? All four adolescents were still at home. I couldn't let go of them. My marriage was still a roller coaster.

The Four Horsemen trotted over the small patches of tenderness that used to show up in waves.

The family saw me as hyper-religious. But Scripture, prayer, and fasting showed me divine invitations. The church helped me raise my children. God showed me truth about myself and my marriage. I learned to be thankful. And I feared my next level of growth would put an even bigger wedge between Richard and me. He thrived on sameness. But our children kept growing, and so did I. In a prayer, I wrote:

Dear Lord, one concern I have is this. As I move forward in my studies (in my continued nurturing and growth), I'm concerned it will bring greater spiritual distance between Richard and me. I give this concern to You, Lord. It's really not mine to bear, is it? Thank You for that peace…that reality…that truth.

Still feeling rejection from my sudden termination, I hoped being with those who loved to learn would help. I had no time to waste. In addition to four years of classes and supervision, I'd study to pass state board exams. My study skills would motivate my high schoolers to get good grades and qualify for scholarships. Then I could work in a counseling practice and have credentials to maintain ethical and trusted services. Most of all, I could provide for my family.

Perpetual disappointments followed me into the classroom. With the exception of a few students, I was in a different stage of life. Studies were designed for those fresh out of college. I had a child in each age category of my Human Growth and Development class.

I felt belittled and disrespected by young professors who supervised and taught me. And I was trying to recover from a male boss's betrayal and being unloved by my husband of nearly three decades. I didn't belong at home, at work, or in this higher-learning environment.

In the course catalog I read the description of a Spiritual Direction class. I enrolled because it included a retreat. Still unsure of this degree program, I wondered if this course would help. I'd never heard of spiritual direction before. Simply put, the difference is that counseling helps clients fix problems whereas spiritual direction is about meeting God in the midst of problems. A spiritual director honors the client's journey and helps accompany them toward transformation. It's the opposite of being authoritative in the counseling room.

This made sense to me because of my focus on deep-soul work. My own post-abortion healing and what I saw while leading groups through the ministry made this class a spark of hope. I didn't want to power over clients with my knowledge and expertise. I wasn't interested in helping people "fix" problems. I couldn't fix my own. But I wanted to show them divine invitations. My soul-searching and prayer journaling drew me.

I could only afford a used copy of *Sacred Companions*,[33] written by my professor, Dr. David G. Benner.[34] I created my own highlights along with existing underlining in the required text. And I was exhausted with efforts, only to watch my marriage fall apart. In my prayer journal, I wrote:

Lord, please turn my deepest needs for my marriage into a hope that produces peace rather than frustration and loss.

I tried to disregard my deepest longings. But Benner's words jumped off the page into the tender places of my soul.

---

33 David G. Benner, *Sacred Companions: The Gift of Spiritual Friendship & Direction* (Downers Grove, IL: InterVarsity Press, 2002).

34 Dr. Benner was my professor when I was a student at Psychological Studies Institute in Chattanooga, Tennessee, and Atlanta. The name has changed to Richmont University: https://www.drdavidgbenner.ca/about/.

"Our spirituality is most clearly expressed in the deep longings that enliven us. Longings, in contrast to mere desires, come from our depths. Longings reflect spirit bubbling up to the surface…. Attending to the spiritual is attending to these stirrings in our depths."[35]

The weekend intensive was a prerequisite to the experiential retreat. When I first met Dr. Benner from the front row of the classroom, he was so opposite of the smug personas I saw in my other classes. His tall, slender frame and distinguished manner oozed with a humble confidence. This professor's Christian faith felt like the kind of peace you'd experience with a Buddhist monk. But to me he was like Mister Rogers in my own neighborhood.[36] With a unique balance of compassion and professionalism, he was unlike any of the male authorities I knew.

Dr. Benner's lectures penetrated my soul just as the words he'd written in his books. This class focused on soul care. His teachings were more about the heart. He said we all are human beings, not "human doings." As if I'd had a full-body massage, the muscles of my soul began to loosen. I was hungry for more.

A month later I joined two other roommates in a cabin. We walked through the wooded pathway and entered a conference room. Soft music and respectful silence greeted the twenty of us as we sat in a circle. Dr. Benner and his wife, Juliet, took their place as our spiritual directors.

The Benners were a mix of Canada and Trinidad. Juliet's clear olive skin, brown eyes, and petite frame complemented her husband's tall frame, fair skin, and blue eyes. Their calm respect reflected their fondness for each other's differences. David led group dialogue, creating space for feelings and experiences. Juliet facilitated meditation using projector slides of Renaissance and European paintings. Together, they provided a

---

35 Benner, *Sacred Companions*, 74.
36 https://www.misterrogers.org

soul-nurturing environment that penetrated the filters of our academic brains and theological mind-sets.

Their natural flow synchronized like ballroom dancers. *So that's what a partnered marriage looks like*, I thought. They practiced realness as a couple. It was the opposite of mine and Richard's disjointed fear and insecurity.

I sat with them during lunch in the cafeteria at a round table with others. Someone asked, "How did you and Juliet meet?" Dr. Benner had a twinkle in his eye as he looked at his wife. It was as if their glances gave each other permission to share the story of their younger selves.

"I met Juliet in my third year of college. I was stunned by her beauty after she arrived on campus from the West Indies. We married two years later and have been together ever since." It wasn't what he said. It was how he said it. "To know Juliet is to love her. Even though our backgrounds were different, she was more spiritually aware than I was."

"But he was more questioning and intellectually aware than me in those days," she added.

Both David and Juliet offered individual time with each student. I was the first to sign up with David and opted to take a walk in the woods.

"Let's walk a little slower, Judy," he said in his Canadian accent.

"Oh, okay," I replied, not aware of my energy. I slowed to match his pace.

"Let's go this way," he said. "We don't want to get too far since our time is limited." The fragrance of nature, the fresh air, and our slower pace opened my senses along with the natural flow of conversation.

"I appreciate your offering a walk in the woods," I began. "I'm thankful to be the first to sign up. I'm learning so much already. From reading your books and being in the class last month…" I didn't notice the speed of my voice as I trailed on.

He spoke with a slow calmness. "Thank you, Judy. I'm touched. This is a gift of dialogue." The pace of his walk and the tempo of his voice invited me to calm my thoughts. Then he asked, "What do you hope to happen with your time here?"

"It's been a huge transition for me. I feel out of place in this program, and it's so hard." I couldn't hold back that familiar lump in my throat and wave of tears. Wait. He had other students after me, and this was a short time. I wiped my nose with my arm.

"I wonder what your tears are saying, Judy," he said.

"I didn't intend to cry. I thought I was over the bucketload of tears I've already cried."

He slowed our pace to a stop and changed our side-by-side visit to a face-to-face. Is this what a father would do? Was he showing me the love of a dad toward his grown daughter? He waited patiently as I poured out a short version of my troubled marriage. He pulled his handkerchief out of his pocket. I accepted. "May I pray for you, Judy?"

"Yes." I waited in the sacred silence on the hiking trail. Dr. Benner wasn't my professor, and he wasn't my dad. He was my spiritual director joining me in God's presence. The smell of autumn and the surround sound of nature triggered deep places in me. His prayer and gift of dialogue calmed me. He paved the way for more divine invitations that weekend.

I signed up for every class he taught in those two years of my program. He mentioned experiences facilitating individual spiritual retreats. After graduation I intended to save money for an individual retreat with him as my guide. I didn't know if I'd still be married. But something had to change.

Chapter 12

INTENTIONAL TURNING

Let us not look back in anger, nor forward
in fear, but around in awareness.
—James Thurber

Some believe criteria for extramarital affairs applies only to direct physical and/or sexual contact with someone other than your spouse. Sexting, pornography, or climax massages don't count. Nor do they recognize a hidden emotional companionship as an affair. But the question to ask is, "Is the friendship or behavior a secret from your spouse?" If yes, it betrays the marital union. Husband and wife must be aligned in their definitions to move beyond their messes. If their therapist is unaware of a secret relationship, couples counseling is in vain.

Couples who are on the verge of divorce or have problems bigger than their counseling sessions may benefit from an intensive program.

Several exist in various formats, from working with a single therapist as a couple to small groups.[37] They may be faith based or professionally facilitated with a room full of couples, but guided to share only with each other.

"Is the friendship or behavior a secret from your spouse? If yes, it betrays the marital union. Husband and wife must be aligned in their definitions to move beyond their messes."

Retrouvaille,[38] a French word meaning *rediscovery*, is a worldwide group-intensive program led by a priest and three volunteer couples. Although they're well-trained leaders who moved beyond their messy marriages within the program, none are professional speakers or counselors. Instead, they read their heartfelt stories with vulnerable transparency. They teach and model a dialogue method that breaks through emotional barriers. They share their partnered journey of awareness, intentionality, and risks. Each couple tells of their crisis, history, recovery, and growth together. Their volunteering alone is evidence of risk, the "r" in our AIR formula. Unbeknownst to every couple until the end, each was lifted up in prayer by a sponsor couple throughout the weekend.

I entered the library and smelled research along with columns of books. A homeschooling mom I knew from the past stood tall in her confidence.

---

37 For an updated list of marriage intensives, go to my website: https://www.messyrelationships.com.

38 With its beginnings in 1977, Retrouvaille is a Christian "multidenominational nonprofit organization with international impact in healing marriages on the verge of divorce": https://www.helpourmarriage.org.

Although our children were the same age, she had continued educating hers. Mine were in public school.

I tried standing just as tall. Like other moms, I prided myself on my children's accomplishments. But in the eyes of homeschoolers, sending your kid to public school is like being on welfare. When I saw her, I held my head high and looked directly into the smugness of her eyes.

"Judy! How are you doing?"

"Hey, I'm glad to see you. How are you?" I hoped the conversation would flow and she wouldn't notice that I'd forgotten her name. I figured I'd remember as she talked about how wonderful her children were. She'd ask about mine. Then I'd move to the next aisle of books.

"Judy. Are you still married?"

"Yes, of course." Goodness, I hardly knew this woman, and she asked if I was still married? Were my problems that evident?

"I mean, are you still married to the same man?" I couldn't believe it. Not once, but twice.

"Yes. Why do you ask?"

"Oh, I saw your husband at the supercenter the other day."

"Oh? When you saw him, did you speak with him?" My tone was naturally condescending. How could she be so tactless?

"No. But I was sure you two were divorced. I was positive someone told me that." Couldn't she have lowered her voice?

"Oh. Do you know who that someone was?"

"No, I don't remember."

"Well, I'm still married to the same man." *Certainly she'll apologize. Our children were little in the same music class. She must be socially awkward. That's it. She has no social filter. That's why she doesn't look embarrassed.* Instead, she stood tall over me as if a schoolteacher were catching her student in a lie. I floundered as I tried to leave respectfully.

"This is a great library, isn't it? I'm finishing up my second master's degree." I tried to one-up her. She was stuck in homeschooling mode. My children were getting a broad and socially valuable education.

"Good for you, Judy."

"Thanks. I'll be in private practice soon." Proud to be on my professional track, I held back from saying more. *And how are YOU modeling growth for YOUR children?* Instead, I obsessed about her arrogant and crude question. Then I wondered. Could this be a sign? Was God using this woman to get my attention? Or was the demise of my marriage that evident?

Next she talked about how one of her brilliant high schoolers got accepted to an Ivy League school. I felt like Charlie Brown listening to the teacher say, "Wha-wha-wha-wha..."

"Yes. This is the only place we could find the level of research he needed. The public library has nothing."

I looked at my watch and acted as if I were late for my next class. "Oh, good to see you. I've gotta go. Bye."

"Bye, Judy. Good to see you too."

I walked out the door into the privacy of my car. I dialed the store's number on my flip phone.

"Supercenter, may I help you?" the female voice answered.

"Yes, would you please page Richard? Sporting goods department."

"Hold please."

A few rings later, he picked up. "Hello?" I didn't recognize his pleasant voice.

"Yeah, I wanted to ask you a quick question." I paused just to hear how quickly his tone changed with me.

"Go on." That horseman spoke.

"I just left the library. And I ran into a homeschool acquaintance from the past."

"Is that why you called? I've got work to do."

"She asked me if I was still married to the same man. Do you know what that's all about?"

"No. Who was it?"

"I can't remember her name, but she's tall and has children the same age as ours. She saw you and was positive someone told her we were divorced."

"Well, I can assure you it didn't come from anyone here."

"Oh?" How could he possibly know what employees or "anyone here" did or didn't do? How arrogant is that?

"Is there any chance you might be acting as if you're a divorced man there? I'm still trying to figure this out."

"My coworkers know we're not doing well. But I've not told anyone we're divorced. I've gotta go."

"Okay." We hung up without goodbyes.

The next day, I searched the bottom of an old filing cabinet. I found the pink cardboard memory box. The rotted rubber band snapped, and I blew off the dust. Wedding cards were in one ziplock bag. In the other were love notes and cards I received in box #2045 when I was a college girl. I opened a few and read the familiar handwriting. It seemed they were to and from someone else. But I wanted our children to know the man their dad used to be and how much he loved me then.

A few weeks later, Richard asked, "What's the name of that marriage intensive weekend you told me about?"

"Hmm. I don't know what you're talking about."

"It starts with an R. Do you remember?"

"Oh, are you thinking of the one for couples in troubled marriages?" I'd forgotten all about Retrouvaille. My persuasion dance didn't help when I wanted us to go years before.

"Yes, that's the one."

"Is it for someone at the supercenter?"

"No, I'm thinking of us."

"Your friend Paul might know." I couldn't imagine him following through. If he wanted to know, he'd ask his friend whom he hadn't seen in years. Paul and his wife used to volunteer.

But he did follow through and registered us. A few weeks later with an inkling of hope, we arrived in a tension-filled room with thirty other couples. One of the three volunteer couples sat next to the priest while each shared portions of their stories. We learned a dialogue method and opened our hearts to each other through guided vulnerability and letter writing.

By Sunday the wicked spell was broken. Including us, couples softened their faces and were able to look into each other's eyes.

The leaders emphasized how vital it was to participate in follow-up sessions. "The next six weeks are even more crucial. Don't expect a weekend intensive to be enough. Most who participate in all the post sessions make it," they said.

But Richard looked at me. "I'm working five of those six sessions."

"Can't you take time off? Isn't it worth saving our marriage?"

"I already took this weekend off, and I'm not going to ask. Besides, the boys have a tournament on two of those weekends. I might be able to go to the last one."

Our children noticed the warmth and tenderness between us. It lasted two weeks. And I had stopped that persuasion dance.

Chapter 13

INTENTIONAL FORGIVENESS

While I dance I cannot judge, I cannot hate, I cannot separate myself from life. I can only be joyful and whole. This is why I dance.

—Hans Bos

W e do more harm than good to embrace the mantra "forgive and forget." Realistically, we won't be able to forget offenses with highly charged emotions attached. Rather, we need to "forgive and remember." Forgiveness doesn't mean we minimize or look the other way. Nor should we pretend the offenses didn't happen. Forgiveness does not mean putting yourself in harm's way. Nor trusting your heart with another only to get it stomped on because of their lack of awareness.

Forgiveness has the potential to mend relationships, but it takes both people to acknowledge the wrong. Relationships begin to heal *only* when one forgives and the other receives it and chooses to make amends.

The work of repairing or creating a new dance can take years. And that work isn't the same as forgiveness. Rather, it involves building trust and being trustworthy. Forgiveness is a prerequisite for relationship healing.

We can forgive without reconciliation. But when we ignore awareness of the offense and come together anyway, we invite the third horseman, Contempt. Many "sweep it under the rug."

Forgiveness is not the same as trusting untrustworthy people. Even if it is your spouse. Forgiveness toward another who won't acknowledge their wrong is truly a divine act. On the cross, Jesus said, "Father, forgive them, for they do not know what they do."[39]

> "The work of repairing or creating a new dance can take years. And that work isn't the same as forgiveness. Rather, it involves building trust and being trustworthy."

It's our lack of awareness (ignorance of our wrongdoing) that harms not only ourselves and others, but the relationship. We must grow in our awareness to have grace for others' ignorance of their wrongs to us. And be aware of how we've unknowingly wronged others.

---

39   Luke 23:34. Jesus made it clear in this passage how harmful and fatal unawareness can be. Our awareness growth is essential throughout our lives. Otherwise, we continue to harm ourselves and others through our ignorance.

The tension was unbearable between Richard and me before the Retrouvaille weekend. Angry letters in my prayer journals helped me be aware of my built-up bitterness.

> *Dear Jesus, this feeling in the pit of my stomach goes beyond the physical… I'm tired of working so hard. I'm tired of apologizing over and again, of my impulsiveness. I'm tired of Richard's harshness and negativity toward me… I'm tired of grieving the loss of my marriage. I'm tired of being unloved by my husband. I just want out, but I don't know where to go. It's too bad my Canada trip is not until June. I'm tired of being alone and unloved and misunderstood and abused. I'm tired of trying to make life work…*

Dr. Benner and I had exchanged emails with confirmed dates for my retreat. During a break at my last class, he'd said, "Judy, I need to let you know ahead of time about the retreat arrangements. Mount Mary's is very Catholic.[40] There'll be statues and icons that you may not be used to."

"That's okay. I want an experience that I'm not used to." At that time, I had thirteen months to save up and plan. I intentionally scheduled the retreat on my twenty-eight-year anniversary. So many of our anniversaries were on the ball fields along with those Four Horsemen. The marriage had become a corpse. He refused to move out. Our teenagers were aware of my resentment. Lyrics of country music songs resonated with me. And I didn't feel like forgiving. But I still wrote in my journals. *"I forgive you for…"* I filled in details of every memory of rejection, abandonment, and betrayal. I had put up with too much for too long. I wasn't getting younger. This marriage was more than toxic. I changed my passwords to creative combinations of the word "forgive."

Then I had a dream.

---

40   http://mountmary.ca/gallery/

I was at an organized party looking at something. A nice handsome-looking man noticed me. He got very close to me physically. We were assigned to two separate group projects painting the cover of a book opaque white. We waited for the paint to dry to do another coat as I tried to clean up the mess.

In one of my classes with Dr. Benner, I learned a way to treat my dreams as prayers.[41] This dream was a pleasant contrast to my daily reality. I titled this dream "The Party." Here's the prayerful questions I wrote.

Dear Lord, how can I go to the party, and what does it represent? Could the good-looking man represent You, Jesus? Your attraction to me? Your desire for me? Your covering and protection of me? Could the separate group project be my distractions? What about the book cover? Is that Your message to me? Am I trying too hard to paint it white? What is this mess I'm trying to clean up? Is this "project" keeping me from the party? Could the "party" be Your invitation to me? Is all I need to do is receive it? Do You require nothing else from me other than to know that I'm loved like I am?

As I pondered questions from my party dream, I became intentional to learn how to dance. Because that's what happens at parties.

My Sunday school student Hannah was a poised ballerina gifted with a tall and slender seventeen-year-old body. She agreed to be my ballet teacher. My lessons were right after her children's class at church.

We started with warm-up exercises with my black leotard, pink tights, ballet slippers, and wraparound skirt. She choreographed the song of my choice with basic and challenging moves. She crafted a few

---

41 Dr. Benner also included the idea of dreams as prayers in his book, *Care of Souls* (Baker Books, 1998), https://www.drdavidgbenner.ca/care-of-souls/.

twirls just right for my body and ability. Learning to dance helped me imagine life beyond grief. It made Scripture come alive beyond the verses in my blue leather Bible.

You have turned for me my mourning into dancing. You have put off my sackcloth and clothed me with gladness. To the end that my glory may sing praise to You and not be silent. O Lord, my God, I will give thanks to You forever.[42]

Each week we reviewed sequenced moves from the previous lesson. Hannah danced the next pattern of pliés, relevés, and pas de chats for me. Her movements were fluid while mine were choppy and insecure. But I practiced every day until it became my version of natural.

I heard music in my head when I woke up. I practiced my twirls from the kitchen to the dining room while waiting for the stove-top vegetables to cook.

"Mom, what are you doing? That's gross," the kids said when I first started.

I ordered them to the other room. "No criticism allowed here." And I kept dancing.

A time or two my daughters encouraged me with, "Wow, Mom. I didn't know you could do that."

In the midst of silent tension, I heard music in my head. During stone-cold looks from Richard, I danced in my imagination. While feeling the dead air of stagnation in our split-foyer home, I danced from one room to the next. Energy filled my soul and flowed from the inside out.

The horseman of Contempt was bearable while my dancing became worship. Our home became a place of movement and aliveness. I imagined Jesus as my partner. The Holy Spirit gave me rhythm, and

42 Psalm 30:11-12

God played the music. I felt positive and energetic during those practice times at home. I was in another dimension during Hannah's lessons at church. Familiar freedom mixed with uncertainty was like the colorful kites flying from the hill of my college campus.

I practiced everything Hannah taught until I could dance in my sleep. My routine became fluid. I no longer thought of the next move. Ballet was in every fiber of my being.

As I talked and planned my Canada retreat months ahead, one of my four adolescent children announced that they wanted to come. I explained why I needed a spiritual retreat away.

"Just imagine Maria in *The Sound of Music*.[43] Do you remember that story? She was the nannie for the Von Trapp family. Remember the scene where she struggled with the tension between her faith and feelings? She left the family and went back to the convent to seek out the mother nun's wisdom."

"Oh, yeah, Mom. We remember that scene and the movie."

"Well, that's what Dr. Benner will do for me. He'll help guide me at this retreat. He said it's 'very Catholic.' So just imagine the convent with an iron gate. I promise you I'll come back refreshed."

"Oh, okay."

Richard and I drove in separate vehicles for the last and only post-Retrouvaille follow-up session. It was a sunny day with white puffy clouds as we all stood outside on the church lawn during the refreshment break. Six weeks had passed since the wicked spell was broken for the nine remaining couples. They were laughing, holding hands, and looking into each other's eyes.

But we were the tenth couple from the original thirty. Richard stood at the far end of the parking lot accompanied by two horsemen,

---

43   *The Sound of Music* (1965), https://www.sound-of-music.com.

Contempt and Stonewalling. I felt awkward standing alone and smiling at others when they glanced my way. The abandonment and sadness gave me clarity. My dancing must have broken the curse for me.

I left early to drive halfway to my retreat. While on the road, I imagined our honeymoon of twenty-eight years before. Was I just as alone on our wedding night? We were young and unaware. We didn't grow together. Or one of us grew and the other was still twenty-three. Or perhaps we were both fourteen in our early twenties.

Six hours later, I checked into the hotel room. I changed into my leotard and pink ballet slippers. I played music on the boom box and danced my routine in between two queen beds and dresser. Space was confining, but I didn't feel alone. Clarity, freedom, and sadness mixed with the energy and movement of my dance.

The next morning, I packed my suitcase and drove another six hours. I crossed the border into Ontario. I entered through the wrought-iron gate entrance of Mount Mary's Retreat Center.[44] It was just like the movie. I imagined feeling like Julie Andrews's character, Maria. It was a quiet convent with a dozen unseen nuns living on the other side of campus. Over a hundred acres of lush green meadows, woodlands, and hiking trails welcomed me. Hardwood trees were scattered throughout the peaceful pastures. It felt holy.

My English Tudor-style cottage had a high-pitched roofline, chimney, and well-manicured lawn. As I walked across the campus to get the key, Sister Janet greeted me. "Would you like me to show you around?"

"Yes, I would. I'm so glad to be here."

We walked together as she pointed to the trails, the small chapel, and the stations of the cross. She showed me the common dining room where I'd eat lunch. "Breakfast is on your own." And she gave me a bag. "The Sisters made this for you." Inside was homemade bread and granola.

---

44   Mount Mary's Retreat Center, http://mountmary.ca.

"Oh, thank you. That's so sweet."

"We also left fresh fruit and farm eggs for you in the refrigerator at the cottage."

"Wow. I really appreciate it. That's so kind. Please let them know I'm thankful."

"I will. We've been praying for you, Judy. Let us know if there's anything you need."

"Thank you."

I walked back to the cottage to unload my luggage and get settled. I unlocked the front door and gasped out loud. "Oh, my! I can't believe it!" I walked into a huge living room with a tiled floor and large area rug. It was a thrilling contrast to the cramped hotel room. This cottage dance floor was God's gift to me, as if He were saying, "Here you are, Judy. Let me turn your mourning into dancing. This is for you."

I couldn't wait to unload my luggage and put on my ballet slippers. I was ready to flow with God's rhythm. All I had to do was roll up the rug and play the music.

Chapter 14

INTENTIONAL RETREAT

*You've gotta dance like there's nobody watching, Love
like you'll never be hurt, Sing like there's nobody
listening, And live like it's heaven on earth.*
—William W. Purkey

Both journal writing and participating in retreats are ways to become clearer about our authentic journey. An individual retreat provides space away from our automatic thoughts, behaviors, and attitudes. A new and peaceful environment refreshes our souls and our brains. Otherwise, we're caught up in the cascade of information overload along with the stress that shortens our lives.

Molecular biologist Elizabeth Blackburn[45] discovered caps on our DNA called telomeres. Like the plastic on the end of a shoelace to keep it

---

45   Elizabeth Blackburn and Elissa Epel, *The Telomere Effect* (New York: Grand Central Publishing, 2017).

from unraveling, telomeres protect our cells from illness and aging. The shorter our telomeres, the quicker we age and more likely we'll be sick. Built-up stress, poor eating habits, lack of sleep, and negative thought patterns affect the length of our telomeres. Likely, those younger-looking peers at our high school reunions have longer telomeres than those who've aged beyond recognition.

We get our souls and our lives recharged when we retreat to a peaceful place away from the daily grind. Some do versions of this through hobbies like yoga retreats, nature hikes, camping, or fishing. But when the intention is spiritual nourishment, those divine invitations are more noticeable. We must move through a pathway of mental torment or boredom before we can tune into our authentic journey.

"An individual retreat provides space away from our automatic thoughts, behaviors, and attitudes. A new and peaceful environment refreshes our souls and our brains. Otherwise, we're caught up in the cascade of information overload along with the stress that shortens our lives."

Distractions, technology, and racing thoughts are enemies to living in the present moment. And they keep us stuck in the messes of our relationships. An open attitude and simple prayer like this can make all the difference: "Here I am, Lord, and I'm ready to be aware." We can breathe in fresh AIR, our formula for awareness, intentions, and risks.

Daylight peeked through the horizontal blinds of my cottage. Scrambled farm eggs and toast refreshed me along with a cup of hot tea as I sat on the front porch. What an oasis for my soul after thirteen months of anticipation!

Dr. Benner and I met each other with memories of previous interactions.

"How are you, Judy?" he said.

I tried answering this simple question. But instead I shared about the darkness of my marriage. It was difficult to explain the highs and lows. "We went to this program called Retrouvaille and opened our hearts on that weekend. Right before coming here, we stood on opposite sides of the parking lot. It was the last and only post-session he attended with me. And yesterday was our anniversary. I'm learning how to dance, and it feels freeing to me. But I'm unsettled."

"Tell me more about yesterday being your anniversary."

"I've felt such grief for so long. I didn't even know if I'd be married when I planned this retreat. I didn't want to feel the same despair from last year's. I can't remember an anniversary where we haven't spent it on a ball field. I thought my wedding day was a sacred time so long ago. Up until yesterday, a small part of me hoped Richard's heart would soften to the point of joining me here. Isn't that crazy?" When I verbalized it out loud to him, my thinking seemed off.

He paused for a moment. "Thank you for sharing that with me. Shall we recognize that as being willful?[46] It's natural to avoid our pain. Yet God wants us to be willing." I was almost offended. Did he think I was coming here to avoid my pain?

As if he read my mind, he said, "It doesn't matter what your motivations were in coming here, Judy. What matters is that you're here. God called you to this place apart from Richard."

---

46 "Willful" in this discussion referred to our human nature to control our circumstances to avoid pain. Another term Dr. Benner used was "social engineering." It's the opposite of living in the flow of life and recognizing divine invitations.

"I need clarity on this retreat."

"What might that look like?"

"I need to know whether or not to pursue divorce. I can't live like this. If I stay in the marriage, it will require a tearing down of who I am. I can't nurture myself *and* the marriage."

"Judy, the opposite is true. You'll be able to give of yourself more when *your soul* is nurtured." I couldn't believe that. He didn't know my story nor what I'd been through.

"I don't know what more I could have done. I hoped God would resurrect a new marriage. How do I seek God as a married woman?" I showed him my Retrouvaille manual that I planned to work through while I was there.

"Now is not the time to focus on that," he said. "Let's put any agendas aside about your marriage. God has called you here in solitude to nurture *your* soul."

"Okay." But I didn't feel okay.

"You don't want to miss what God has for you now. Let's stay in the present and be open. Be aware of His invitations to you. And be aware of your responses."

"Oh, I have no problem trusting God. I usually say yes to His invitations. That's why I learned to dance. I'm tired of grieving for so many years. He's turning my mourning into dancing." I hoped he understood. "You see, I brought my ballet slippers, and my Sunday school student taught me a routine. I want to dance here. When I opened the door to this cottage for the first time, I cried. This large living room is my dance floor! It's God's gift to me. I could hardly believe it!" I teared up just telling him all this.

The next four days we met in the mornings. He listened to my previous day's experiences. Then he asked questions to help me be more aware and intentional.

"Judy, be aware of any entitlement that comes up for you. Don't look too far back in history. Instead, look to the present moment."

"Okay." I wrote his questions in my journal.

- If God has been inviting you from mourning to dancing, what has been blocking you from receiving?
- Ask God to help you hear His invitation to life clearly.
- Leave yourself open while you're here.
- Ask yourself, *What keeps me from letting go?*
- Ask, *How can I say a vibrant yes to God's invitations?*
- Keep attentive, both to divine invitations and your responses throughout the day.

I carried my journal and pen everywhere. I hiked the trails with these questions in my heart looking for God's peace. I was intentional to be aware of my energy. When I was tired, I took a nap. When I was curious, I took a walk. When I was hungry, I ate. When I had an idea, I wrote.

One day at the end of my hiking trail I walked into an open landscaped lawn. I saw something about a hundred yards away that piqued my curiosity. As I walked closer, I discovered a massive structure. I laughed and ran toward it, an unexpected divine invitation!

The structure had seven wide terraced steps on three sides. Three concave panels larger than a three-story building overarched the stage. Spotlights on the top of each panel illuminated intricate mosaic images of the Father, Son, and Holy Spirit. The steps led me to a wooden floor engraved in marble. It was a giant outdoor art gallery! Lush green treetops framed a light-blue canvas with brushstrokes of white fluffy clouds. At this Byzantine-style altar, God said, "Judy, dance with Me." I took off my shoes as my body moved to the rhythm in my head. I laughed until I cried. I wrote this list in my journal.

No music
Lighthearted
Unsure at first
Comfortable as I danced on
Giddy
Laughter
Joyful
Fun
Confident
Privileged
Awestruck
Overwhelmed
Worshipful
Free
Blessed
Beloved

In my ecstasy I realized the convent was close by. What would the nuns think if they saw me dance? I'd better ask permission. Feeling the soft, cool grass under my bare feet, I walked to the small manor house with tall chimneys and steep rooflines. I entered the vestibule and knocked. One of the nuns opened the door.

"Is Sister Janet there?" I felt like a little kid in the neighborhood who wanted to play.

"Yes. Would you like to come in?"

"Oh, no thank you. My name is Judy. And I want to thank you for the granola and farm eggs. They were delicious." Then Sister Janet walked to the door and smiled.

"Hi, Judy. How are you?"

"I'm doing great. I didn't realize this stage was here." I pointed behind me.

"Oh, that's the Pilgrimage Altar. Hundreds of people gather here for the Annual Marian Pilgrimage. Most are clergy, volunteers, staff, and nuns."

"Oh, I had no idea," I said. "Is it all right for me to bring my music and dance there?"

"We saw you were already dancing."

"Yes, I hope that was okay. I didn't know anyone was watching."

"Is it a liturgical dance?"

"Yes. May I bring my boom box and dance more?"

"Yes. And I hope you don't mind that we watch."

"No, I don't mind. Thank you." And I gave her a big hug.

I ran back to the cottage for my dance clothes and music. I walked the wide stairs and felt like a child with unhindered twirls, skips, and jumps. I laughed and cried until I could dance no more. From my journal, I wrote.

I danced a good hour into the night. I even lingered on until the stars began to shine so I could dance for You then. I fully enjoyed the laughter You gave me while I danced. You were everywhere all around me, Lord, as I twirled and moved to the rhythm of the music. "You have turned for me my mourning into dancing." Lord, I'll carry Your light into the darkness. I'll continue to dance in the little cottage and meet You there too.

The next day I got up after a peaceful sleep with an unconventional thought that I tried to ignore. I didn't need to take any more risks. I had already risked asking the nuns if I could dance. What would Dr. Benner think?

I tried ignoring it as I ate fruit and granola. The thought wouldn't go away as I sipped my hot tea on the front porch. *Is this Your divine invitation?* I asked.

He's going to think I'm crazy, I thought as I pulled my hair back in a ponytail and put on my leotard and tights. I fastened my ballet slippers and grabbed my boom box. I left a note on the front door. "Join us at the Pilgrimage Altar." I practiced before Dr. Benner came and watched. Just as he respected my tears during our walk in the woods, he honored my dancing as if it were worship. It wasn't a performance.

While walking in the woods again, I talked with him about my marital concerns.

"Yes, my soul has been nurtured on this retreat. But how can I go back to the oppression in my marriage? Here's what I read from Scripture this morning. *What more could have been done to My vineyard that I have not done in it? Why then, when I expected it to bring forth good grapes, did it bring forth wild grapes?*[47]

He said something radical. "Judy, God's love is not enough."

"What?" I couldn't hide my reaction.

"God's love is a gift to each of us. But it's not enough. He gives it to us. For it to be enough, we must receive it. You can only receive it for yourself. But you can't receive it for Richard."

What was I mourning? Was it the death of a marriage? Or the death of my false self showing up as overcompensating for my marriage? I can only receive God's gift for myself.

---

47   Isaiah 5:4

Chapter 15

INTENTIONAL VISION

We played the flute for you, And you did not dance;
We mourned to you, And you did not lament.
—Matthew 11:17

Some of us remember a train diagram with a caboose and smoke-stack engine showing the irrelevance of feelings in our faith experiences.[48] The underlying message is that calm feelings during life's hardships reflect faith. But depression, anxiety, fear, or sadness represent sin. As kids, we may have heard our parents say, "Stop crying or I'll give you something to cry about." Young boys who've grown up to be men have believed, "Big boys don't cry. Shake it off." This dogma paves the way for the Four Horsemen to come trotting into our marriages.

---

48   You can find the purpose, diagram, and verses attached to this illustration at
      https://campusministry.org/article/napkins-top-discipleship-diagrams.

We've learned how to ignore our feelings and our bodies. Yet God's design for our humanity is to grow in awareness of our authentic selves. We must pay attention to our gut. Our emotions are valuable. They are temporary messengers to our souls. We miss out on wisdom and growth if we ignore their messages.

> "We must pay attention to our gut. Our emotions are valuable. They are temporary messengers to our souls. We miss out on wisdom and growth if we ignore their messages."

As an analogy, most of us stay in a hotel as temporary guests when we travel. If you're like us, you'll stay in a RV camper or cabin. But we live in our homes as permanent residents. When we allow emotions to become permanent residents rather than temporary guests, we create many of the symptoms that lead to depression or anxiety. Our automatic thoughts keep us unaware of how we're reinforcing limited beliefs about ourselves and others.

After dancing at the outdoor altar, I didn't want to dance in the dark cottage anymore. I felt open and freer under the blue sky and warm sunshine. Initially, I was overcome with the unexpected invitation to dance in the large living room. But the more extravagant place to dance was the outdoor altar. I compared the two.

Cottage Dancing	Altar Dancing
Dark	Light
Enclosed	Open air
Limited space	More than enough space
Private	Endless sky
Facilities	No facilities
A place to rest and sleep	No place to sleep
Common	Extravagant
Protection from elements	Natural life
Designed for family	No protection from elements
Provision for life	Designed for many
Refrigerator, stove, food	No provision for life
Smooth floor	Rough and smooth tile (wood and marble)

I asked myself questions. If the cottage represents my marriage, does the outdoor altar represent ministry? Do I need them both? I wrote in my journal:

Dear Lord, what do I do if Richard continues to erode away the precious gift You've given us? Or maybe a more appropriate question for me now is this. How am I eroding away this precious gift You've given me? Have I eroded in the dark cottage? Is it my unaware "social engineering" issues that have kept my marriage in such despair?

Dr. Benner was so gracious to use the term "social engineering." He helped me be aware of my natural control tendencies. It was like I had written the script and hired a stage crew. But the cast wasn't playing their parts. I was mourning my certainty about how God would answer my prayers. I still didn't know the next step after my retreat. But I left with contrasted dancing in the dark cottage and the outdoor altar.

I tried to accept the inevitable divorce. But this was a journey of awareness. I scanned for spiritual malware in my beliefs, attitudes, and automatic thoughts. God invited me to be intentional about letting go. This was a monumental risk of changing our family tree. Yet I still asked these questions.

- Can I stay with a husband unwilling to let go of an emotional affair?
- How do I accept Richard as he is?
- How do I stop my agenda of change?
- How can I have freedom in this marriage?

Okay. I realize I have "social engineering" issues. Dr. Benner said, "It's not circumstances that destroy a marriage, but it's the individuals who decide."

My left brain wanted answers. My right brain danced. I embraced the integration and took deep breaths of air when my reptile brain got fired up. My awareness was crucial. More messages came through the temporary guests of my soul. I left the Canada retreat and drove back to the "dark cottage" of my marital life—an eerie contrast.

"My left brain wanted answers. My right brain danced. I embraced the integration and took deep breaths of air when my reptile brain got fired up. My awareness was crucial."

I consulted with divorce attorneys and met with a local spiritual director in addition to my beloved counselor, Penny. I took my state board exams and continued my part-time job as post-abortion director. Among the tasks of training leaders and volunteers, facilitating retreats became my favorite part of the job.

I received further training through Rachel's Vineyard,[49] an international retreat format for those touched by abortion. Starting Friday and ending Sunday with a memorial service, it helps heal parents and honors those who've died through abortion. Guided meditations, Scripture, music, and experiential involvement provide a depth of transformational healing. Rachel's Vineyard was a powerful prologue to the Bible study groups developed through my work at the pregnancy center.

At a training conference months before, I met a group of leaders who invited me to be their support counselor. They agreed to fly me to Kansas if I volunteered my time. I said yes, eager to disconnect from the toxic atmosphere in our home.

Just in case there was a divine invitation, I packed my ballet slippers, leotard, and tights. Richard threatened to leave during an argument before I left. "You can count on me not being here when you get back."

As I waited at the airport terminal, I pulled out my transient sacred space from my carry-on bag. I wrote in my journal: *Am I okay if he's not there when I come home? Am I relieved? How can I provide for my teenagers at home?* I wrote lists of benefits and liabilities of legally staying in the marriage. I needed health insurance, and he was still the primary breadwinner. I asked myself, *How can I detach from the stuff I'm leaving behind for now and be present for this retreat?*

As I looked up from my writing, I watched people coming and going with their "hellos" and "goodbyes." Every loving embrace between husband and wife reminded me of how alone I was.

---

49   Rachel's Vineyard is a powerful experiential retreat founded by Dr. Theresa Burke and facilitated by well-trained volunteers. with global outreach. http://www.rachelsvineyard.org.

"Ladies and gentlemen, Flight #158 is now ready to board."

I put the journal back and stood up with the strap around my shoulder while holding my boarding pass. I joined the others as I inched my way to the front of the line. The attendant reached for my boarding pass and the next passenger's just as smoothly as a cashier scans for grocery items. Without looking up she said, "Have a good flight."

"Thank you." Was she saying that to me? Or the other passenger? I walked the aisle toward the aircraft to join the line again. The flight attendant stood at the narrow entry with her automatic smile and programmed "Enjoy your flight."

I settled in my window seat and buckled into the pressurized cabin. Rather than watching people, I took out my journal before stowing my bag under the seat in front of me. An elderly couple sat in the two seats next to me.

Throughout the flight they snuggled next to each other. She laid her head on his shoulder. He put his hand on her lap. They reminded me of what I'd never have. I was nearly fifty. Why couldn't I let go of a dead marriage?

When the plane began its descent, I glanced at the couple again. I avoided eye contact and guessed they were in their eighties. I put my journal back in the carry-on and closed my eyes during landing. The aircraft came to a full stop at the terminal, and I unlocked my seatbelt. *This couple should be congratulated*, I thought. *I'd better say something*.

"I noticed you two have such a loving connection with each other."

They smiled.

"How long have you been married?" Immediately I realized my assumption. What if they were not married?

"Oh, we're newlyweds," the woman said. They smiled and nodded in agreement. "We're still on our honeymoon! We've been married for thirteen years."

"Wow. Congratulations! It blessed me to see you two."

I inched my way in line out of the plane to meet the volunteer who drove me to the hotel. I had just enough time to get settled before the retreat began. The weekend was filled with divine moments for others and me. I danced at the memorial service as if it were the outdoor altar. And in quiet moments at the hotel, I thought of that elderly couple on the plane.

When I came home Richard was still there. It wasn't long before another argument escalated with threats and raised voices. My arm was caught in the door.

Our son to whom we promised never to get divorced had grown to be an adult-sized teenager. This time he ran up the stairs ready to fight his dad to protect me.

"What's going on?" he asked with anger of his own.

"Everything's all right," Richard said.

Then he looked at me. "Mom? Are you all right?"

"No, son. I'm not…"

Chapter 16

INTENTIONAL MOVEMENT

*Then young women will dance and be glad, young men
and old as well. I will turn their mourning into gladness;
I will give them comfort and joy instead of sorrow.*
—Jeremiah 31:13

There's mystery in the idea of two becoming one[50] when a new bride and groom walk down the aisle to say, "I do." And they may agree. But one may think, *Yes, we two are one. And I'm the one.* Oftentimes the bride agrees. She may also be thinking, *Yes, we two are one. And you're the one.*

If they both continue the power/control dance, with assumptions that she orbits around his world, she stifles his character development. He's too comfortable to empathize or grow beyond his adolescent ways of thinking. And she may become depressed, angry, and resentful. She

---

50 Mark 10:8-9. This passage is quoted often in Christian wedding ceremonies.

loses her authentic self with illusions of "social engineering." Both miss out on growing up.

As with all living things, we're designed to grow. It takes two adults to have a partnered marriage. There needs to be balance between "me" and "we." And it requires respect of both individuals and the relationship.

"If they both continue the power/control dance, with assumptions that she orbits around his world, she stifles his character development. He's too comfortable to empathize or grow beyond his adolescent ways of thinking. They both miss out on growing up."

The book *The Verbally Abusive Relationship*[51] by Patricia Evans has given me profound understanding both in my counseling office and personal life. Even though it was first published in the early 1990s, it is included in counselor training programs today.[52] She clarifies two different realities which I've identified as the submission/control dance that keeps us from our authentic selves. Reality One is our lack of awareness over childish ways of thinking. Reality Two is our growing awareness into mature thinking. And it takes two adults who continue to grow beyond their childhood "reality" to get beyond messy marriages.

Here's how the realities compare:

---

51 Patricia Evans, *The Verbally Abusive Relationship* (Avon, MA: Adams Media Corp., 2010), http://www.verbalabuse.com.

52 Not only has Patricia Evans been on Oprah, but her book was also included in a training program I took through the Zur Institute: https://www.zurinstitute.com/intimateviolencecourse.html.

Reality One vs. Reality Two
Disregard vs. Validation
Hostility vs. Goodwill
Control vs. Intimacy
Manipulation vs. Mutuality
Competition vs. Partnership
Unequal vs. Equal

Christian author Leslie Vernick is making an impact on educating clergy, pastors, and women who value scriptural principles through her book *The Emotionally Destructive Marriage.*[53] Author Lundy Bancroft articulates his experiences working with over a thousand "abusers" as an intervention counselor in *Why Does He Do That?*[54] Several of my male clients have become more aware because of insights from this book.

To break the pattern of the power/control dance, we must recognize the "normalcy" of cultural, religious, and family emotional abuse.

The legal divorce hinged on my getting a full-time job. I sat across from Pam's desk at the pregnancy center. She had been my boss for six years. At an earlier time in my life, I was her new volunteer.

"Pam, I need to let you know that I've been struggling in my marriage for years."

"Oh, Judy. I'm sorry to hear this."

I needed to tell her before she read about it in the newspaper. "We'll be getting a divorce."

---

53 Leslie Vernick, *The Emotionally Destructive Marriage* (Colorado Springs: Waterbrook Press, 2013). Find more from her website: https://leslievernick.com.
54 Lundy Bancroft, *Why Does He Do That?* (New York: The Berkley Publishing Group, 2002). You can find out more through his website: http://lundybancroft.com.

My growth challenged my conservative interpretation of Scripture. And I didn't expect her to understand. But my explanation of "why" didn't fit the biblical criteria for divorce.[55] She hired my replacement, a volunteer I previously trained to lead post-abortion groups. After I left my position, the Rachel's Vineyard retreats were no longer part of the post-abortion program. Their theology didn't fit the evangelical ministry.

I applied to every counseling group practice and community mental health agency in town. I had my license as a counselor but no job. I taught a divorce parenting class and even played the piano for a friend's Christmas party to earn income. I deposited checks from a minimum-wage retail job during Christmas. I got a temporary position at an insurance company making fourteen dollars an hour. Then I joined a freshly licensed young counselor in private practice. But my four clients a week weren't enough to retain an attorney.

I cried the day someone handed me five $100 bills. I prayed for the right buyers for my beloved piano. That money along with what I got for my engagement ring paid the mortgage that month. I cried more about the piano.

Judgmental looks came from some friends and church acquaintances. I didn't know how I'd pay next month's mortgage. The book of James says that pure and undefiled religion is helping widows and orphans in their trouble.[56] Within our culture, I wondered if that would apply to my situation of being neglected and having four teenagers to care for? The church helped others through their benevolence fund. I'd never been so needy before. This was the darkest season of my life.

I sat across from Pastor Kevin's desk as he listened to my story. His compassion gave me hope, and I asked about the church's financial support. "You'll need to share with the benevolence committee on

---

55 Most believe divorce is permitted in cases of abuse, abandonment, or adultery. Some conservative Christians only consider a divorce "biblical" when the marriage contract is broken through a spouse's adultery.

56 James 1:27, teaching about true religion.

Wednesday. I don't have any part of that. Let them know you've met with me and the steps you've already taken."

"Oh, thank you." I had such relief as I walked out of his office. Then I went to the youth center to wait for my boys. Other adolescents were playing ping-pong. I felt such lighthearted relief as I watched them play.

"Do you know how to play round-robin?" I asked.

"No, we haven't heard of it. Show us." They handed me the paddle. A dozen others joined in. I felt energy, laughter, and fun as I had as a college girl. My sons joined in. "Wow, Mom. I didn't know you could do that."

A few days later I met with the committee to present my needs. Like a defendant awaiting a jury's deliberation, I waited for their decision. Two male deacons approached me, and one of them said something like this: "Judy, we can't imagine your marriage this way. We've known your family for years. We understand you and Richard are having difficulties. But since you don't have biblical grounds for divorce, it goes against church policy to support you. We're so sorry. I know this is not what you wanted to hear."

I felt the pit in my stomach before he finished his first sentence. But the pit felt like lead as I bowed my head and said a soft, "Thanks anyway." The boys tried to convince me their dad had changed since he started going to church.

A few days later, one of the pastors knocked on my door.

"Judy, I'm so sorry. I heard about the decision of the benevolence committee. This isn't much, but I wanted to give it to you. Please don't let the staff or others know." He handed me two $100 bills.

"Thank you." I didn't turn my face away. Instead I showed my tears of gratitude. "This helps a lot. I can hardly speak."

My friend's church helped with food, and my mom gave what she could. Nine months of a restraining order ended with my signature before a judge. Richard signed the week before. The legal divorce was final when I walked out of the courtroom. I felt grief all over again.

———————

At my temporary job, I met Ann, who fascinated me by her world travels and competitive ballroom dancing. I thought of her as a wise woman since she was a generation older than me with white hair and a confident posture. "I'd love to see videos of your competition if you have any. I've taken ballet lessons, but I'd love to learn ballroom." And I couldn't hold back my curiosity. "How long have you been single, Ann?"

"Oh, for decades!" She chuckled.

"I'm trying to adjust as a freshly divorced woman myself. And I just started my counseling practice. Tell me, how did you get into ballroom dancing?" During breaks, she showed me her videos and directed me to the best instructors in town. She invited me to the studio where she took lessons. I met her at the dance studio when I went to my first beginner group class.

After the teaching, dim lights reflecting from the rotating disco ball invited dancers to synchronize with Michael Bublé's "Haven't Met You Yet."[57] The large speaker played one foxtrot after another. Ladies lined up and paired with the next gentleman for their turn around the room. Bows and curtsies signaled her drop-off, with him scurrying to the next one in line.

Females always outnumbered males. The foxtrot or waltz lines were preludes to the Latin and smooth random dancing throughout the evening. Some couples danced only with each other while others switched partners.

Besides Ann, I met other girlfriends with a passion for ballroom. At times we were asked to dance by a poised and confident teacher. They

———————

57   Bublé's lighthearted music and upbeat tunes: https://www.youtube.com/ watch?v=1AJmKkU5POA.

made us look graceful and flowing. But if we got an insecure beginner, we did our best to back-lead.

Male dancers came in all shapes and sizes, young and old, skilled and clumsy. They were sweaty and clean, pleasant and embarrassing, competent and sloppy. We knew them by their dance. Pierre was the best bolero dancer. Markel made the West Coast swing look easy. Miguel was a natural merengue dancer, and Jeff could waltz like no other. We developed unique chemistry with different partners and dance styles over others.

Ballroom etiquette made physical connection with the opposite sex a healthy supply of oxytocin without dating. Male partners became friends and acquaintances.

When I got a full-time job as a triage counselor, I was on call 24/7 during my shift. My position was a gatekeeper for those needing inpatient care. I was trained as a mandatory certified clinician with credentials to admit patients who were a danger to themselves or others. This full-time position was ideal for building my private practice. Sometimes I wouldn't get any crisis calls for a week at a time. And other weeks were back-to-back with intense cases.

It was common for me to drive to emergency rooms, foster or group homes, or schools to assess children under the age of seventeen experiencing a mental health crisis. Some were in "regular families" struggling with severe mental illness. I determined the next level of treatment whether it was for counseling or admission to a psychiatric hospital. The scenarios made me appreciate the problems I had at home as I bore the emotional pain of my sons and daughters.

Not only were cases oppressive and dark, but I also relived each one by writing extensive case notes to satisfy required documentation. Visits to teenagers in their hospital rooms as they recovered from bruises from a suicide attempt became agonizing realities. The position made me susceptible to compassion fatigue. For my mental well-being, I needed lighthearted fun.

Dancing became a necessity. It was a way to balance my exposure to the darkest shadows of humanity. Movement, laughter, and fun relieved my body of stress and refreshed my mind.

A sudden exit from a dance to respond to a call made it difficult to conceal my profession. In social settings I became a magnet to folks who wanted my advice about their problems. But I wanted to be another dancer having fun.

One time as I sat down to watch the half-time showcase, a nice-looking man walked toward me. I had danced a couple rounds with him in the waltz line. As a beginner, I couldn't talk and dance at the same time. It was normal not to know a person's name.

"Is anyone sitting here?"

"No, have a seat. I'm Judy."

"My name's Joe. It looks like you're having fun."

"Yes. I started taking private lessons. How long have you been dancing?"

"I started last year about this time. My doctor said I needed to have fun. So I took group lessons." As our new conversation continued, it flowed into his next statement. "By the way, I have bipolar disorder."

"Oh." Why would this guy tell me that? But he didn't ask advice. Instead, we exchanged other information similar to how Ann and I had at the office.

It was the highlight of my week to take lessons, go to dance parties, and meet new people. I experienced movement, creativity, music, rhythm, and emotionally safe partnerships. Ballroom was like sparks of light away from the dark grief of my former life. It felt liberating.

I met another friend in the foxtrot line, Marcia. She was behind me as we waited for our turn. While inching along, she asked, "How long have you been dancing?"

"Oh, for months." I had progressed quickly at the intermediate level. She was a beginner with her newfound love of ballroom.

"Wow, you're good," she said.

"Thanks. I love it. It balances me like nothing else." And I shared about my work in crisis counseling. She shared about her executive position in her career.

"What about you?" I asked. "How long have you been dancing?"

"Oh, I just started private lessons two weeks ago. I've wanted to do this for a long time. I love it."

"It'll grow on you. You're doing great." And I took my turn at the front of the line with Pierre. She paired with Markel.

Marcia's first marriage had the same Four Horsemen as mine. Neither of us knew how to date. She had raised two grown sons, now with families of their own. My two sons still lived at home. I admired her lifestyle of hiking and adventures. She looked younger than she was. Her knee-length dresses accentuated her athletic figure and muscular legs.

For us, ballroom dancing brought attention to the Princess parts of ourselves. The Cinderella and Sleeping Beauty stories came alive. Sometimes we tested the flow of our new dresses while waiting in line.

It was a pleasant family-type community. Dance partners were as old as eighty-something to as young as nine. We developed friendships with both sexes. Some girlfriends became soul sisters while others remained acquaintances. Most of the guys were proper gentlemen. Some were married couples, but most were single. Motivations ranged from health reasons to pure enjoyment. Some were overcoming depression or recovering from divorce or widowhood. The academic world and work environment didn't feel like places I belonged. And I no longer felt connected in my church. But I loved the lighthearted mood on the dance floor of joyful laughter mixed with occasional toe stepping.

I was responsible for two adolescents at home. Two others had left to create intense lives of their own. And my heartache continued.

Except on the dance floor.

Chapter 17
RISK OF FUN

When a body moves, it's the most revealing thing.
Dance for me a minute, and I'll tell you who you are.
—Mikhail Baryshnikov

tudies about the neurological effects of dancing give evidence of mental health benefits.[58] The elderly can reduce their risk of dementia. Also, dancing helps patients with Parkinson's disease. Moving the body with rhythm and music actually triggers the brain's sensory and motor circuits.

When we dance, we dissipate built-up cortisol, the stress hormone. We increase our serotonin, the feel-good hormone. Our memory and moods improve. It happens in combination of listening to music tunes while moving along with the beat. Thanks to the technology of brain

58 The Dancing Brain: Structural and functional Signatures of Expert Dance Training: https://www.ncbi.nlm.nih.gov/pmc/articles/PMC5711858/.

imaging, we gain a clear picture of neural regions being activated for those who dance. We know that problem-solving, memory retention, and creativity improve with dancing.

"When you move your body to the rhythm and melody of music, you're nurturing your mental and emotional wellness."

In short, dancers strengthen their neuronal connections. Those connections increase new learning and mental focus. When you move your body to the rhythm and melody of music, you're nurturing your mental and emotional wellness. Complex mental and physical coordination improves. And it doesn't matter, whether it's belly dancing, ballroom, or ballet.

Our dance community gathered along with multitudes for "Swing Fest" at the park downtown with a live band on stage. A portable wooden dance floor was big enough to hold less than 10 percent of the people who tried dancing on it.

A few church friends who knew me as the dance evangelist were there. After dancing with several others, I scanned the crowd and spotted Joe. But, I pretended I didn't notice him. When the trumpets began their intro to "The Chattanooga Choo Choo,"[59] Joe reached his hand out to me for a swing. He motioned a "hurry" to stake our spot on the floor. When that number ended and another swing began, we thanked each other and moved to the next familiar dancer.

---

59   You can find out more about Glen Miller's Big Band tune from 1941 on NPR music news Feb. 10, 2017: https://www.npr.org/2017/02/10/514522626/how-chattanooga-choo-choo-became-the-worlds-first-gold-recordo.

My church and dance friends knew my choice not to date for an entire year after my divorce. And I could turn down offers without fear of rejecting the person who asked. I concluded that temporary dance partners were not dates.

I expected another offer to dance when Joe approached me again. Instead, he said, "Uh, I was wondering if you might be interested…"

"Huh?" I couldn't hear since the music was too loud.

He got closer and spoke louder. "There's a special dance next Friday night…"

"What?" This time I pretended.

"Let's walk over here." We walked away from the loudspeakers. "There's a dance next Friday, and I'm wondering if you'd like to go?"

"You know I've told you that I'm not dating anyone at this point."

"I know. I remember you telling me. But I don't consider this a date. I've taken lessons from the owner, and she does a good job with this event once a year. It's a semiformal dance. And it's not the kind of thing to attend without a partner. I took my friend Shirley last year. But this year she's going with someone else. So, if you'd like to go with me, we would just be hanging out. But we'd be dancing with each other the whole evening."

"Hmm. I appreciate your asking but…"

"Take your time to think about it. It's a time to enjoy an event and have someone to dance with."

"Oh, okay. I'll think about it." I tried to hide my excitement. *Do I take this minor "risk"? I can easily say no.*

I walked closer to the action so I'd get asked to dance by others I knew. But I felt the pitter-patter of curiosity. And my church friends wouldn't know since I turned down another "date" from that group.

When the dance was over, Joe looked my way and I looked his. We walked toward each other. "Okay. I'll go with you as long as it's not a date. I'll pay my own way. I'll just ride with you there."

As a social dancer, I had more fun than I ever had hanging out with my Bible study friends. Since we were "just friends" at the semiformal event, I agreed to attend another. The next one was a formal dance that reminded me of prom. We walked into a familiar ballroom. Crystal chandeliers hung from beams in the cathedral ceiling. It was the same venue I spoke at when I shared my public testimony for the first time.

We sat at a round table with servers, making me feel like British royalty. A live band played on a similar stage that I spoke at with my 4 x 6-inch index cards. The large wooden dance floor was the centerpiece. Joe wasn't my only dance partner that evening, but when we rode to and from the event, we sat in the backseat of the car along with four others.

It had been over a year since my Canada retreat. While Dr. Benner taught another intensive for a different class of students, I met him again. This time I stayed at a nearby retreat center. My ballet dancing had transformed into ballroom. I needed insight about relationships and boundaries. Among all my other dance partners, I was cautious about my friendship with Joe.

Dr. Benner gave me more questions to reflect on at the Jesuit retreat center. It was a sacred time to be away from home, work, and social life and felt just as profound as my Canada retreat, only in a different way. I wrote in my journal:

Dear Lord, I feel truly blessed in this time of retreat with You. I feel energized and full of life. Thank You for Dr. Benner's observation of my growing vitality. He compared it to the very painful dark place when we met fifteen months ago… May this vitality spread to my children and others You bring my way.

Although Dr. Benner wasn't a dancer, he resonated with my passion because he loved sailing in a similar way. I went to the library during my retreat and read an article he had written months before. But it was current in the magazine.

In the article, he described contemplative prayer as a dance. Our partner is the Holy Spirit. It takes place between Scriptures and silence. He used the same metaphors I experienced in real life. The dance floor was the place to forget what you learned before. Allow change in your dance steps to match the "rhythm of the Word and the music of silence."[60]

We talked about my growing counseling practice. I felt both unsettled and drawn to counseling couples. But how would pastors or prospective clients trust me as a couple's counselor since I was divorced?

He said something like this: "Judy, allow your counseling practice to grow out of your being. Remember you are a human being. Don't get caught up in living as a 'human doing.' Let your counseling reflect your grounding in truth. Remember that you are a person rather than a theology."

I gazed at a picture of Joe and me someone had taken at the ballroom. He was a man of mystery and depth. But he was so open and lighthearted. Without being vulnerable to a romance with anyone, Joe would continue to be my friend. And we had chemistry on the dance floor.

---

60 David G. Benner, "Being With God: The Practice of Contemplative Prayer" Conversations 4:2, Fall 2006, p. 9.

Chapter 18

RISK OF CHANGE

And the day came when the risk to remain tight in a
bud was more painful than the risk it took to blossom.
—Anais Nin

Times of being alone to recharge and gain perspective can be a healthy dose of solitude. And whether we're energized as introverts or extroverts, our biggest enemy is an isolated life. When we continually hide ourselves from others, we're cut off from significant mirrors that help us grow.

In addition to Gottman's Four Horsemen, I'd name a fifth one called Isolation. Marriages and individuals are at high risk of losing their authentic selves through hiding or avoiding significant relationships. Intentional moves to de-isolate are absolutely necessary to get beyond messy relationships. A first step toward our authentic journey may be to participate in support groups. If that's too risky, start with individual counseling. Reading books is helpful. But nothing can replace the value of face-to-face relationships to get beyond the dances of the "disasters." We must be aware and intentional before we can take the risk of growth.

Even though the Four Horsemen are toxic, they're normal for some. Criticism, defensiveness, stonewalling, and contempt in a marriage are attitudes that set up unhealthy alignments between parent and child. One or both parents confide with son or daughter as if they were a surrogate spouse. When I hear stories of clients who've taken the role of "savior" or "counselor" in their family of origins, I realize it's no wonder they struggle with anxiety and depression. Author Dr. Patricia Love[61] calls this emotional incest. Patterned attitudes get passed throughout the family tree. It's crucial that we become aware of the Four Horsemen even though they may be the only "normal" we know.

Being a counselor has helped me have grace for myself as well as others. I've never counseled a mother in my office who hasn't struggled with guilt over parenting her children. And I've come to believe, to some extent, that guilt is part of parenting. But, if we remain unaware, our chronic guilt can harm our children.

Guilt-motivated parenting conditions our sons and daughters to synchronize the manipulation/control dance. Those who've learned to manipulate and claim victim mentality as their world view, will likely choose guilt-driven partners. Of course, this learned dance keeps our children from becoming the responsible adults we desire for them to be. Instead, our lack of awareness conditions them to bypass their growth process. It's crucial that we continue our growing awareness throughout our lives.

Our task is to "forgive and remember." Then let it go. When we're not forgiven by another, we can still forgive ourselves. Many of my

---

61   Dr. Patricia Love, *The Emotional Incest Syndrome* (New York: Bantam Books, 1991). The book is not as heavy as its title. Rather it will give perspective and hope in parenting and relationships. Here's more from her website: http://www.patlove.com/index.php/books-2/.

clients "don't want to go there," meaning the previous dark times. But we need to remember well enough to glean life lessons from our regrets.

"Marriages and individuals are at high risk of losing their authentic selves through hiding or avoiding significant relationships. Intentional moves to de-isolate are absolutely necessary to get beyond messy relationships."

Counselors can help clients de-isolate, scan for spiritual malware, and gain perspective. We can learn how to take deep breaths and thank God for the wisdom we've learned through our struggling humanity. After all, in the history of mankind, only one was born into this world who lived a perfect life. And we're not Jesus. Again, we're reminded of ancient truths through New Testament texts... *in everything give thanks...*[62]

As mentioned before, true guilt is a temporary emotion with the purpose of turning in the opposite direction. We need to process through difficult memories to dissipate shame. Yet we're not alone. Instead, we're in the sacred space of divine invitations. We're reminded of our deep breaths of AIR: awareness, intentionality, and risks.

I missed playing my piano. And I didn't need to worry about which daughter would get my wedding ring. The four were emerging into their young adulthoods. While I was more than ready to live my new life, they were figuring out their new "normal." Their growth was inevitable, and so was mine.

---

62 1 Thessalonians 5:18

"Mom, you're different."

"What do you mean?"

"Well, you dress differently. You're dancing. You played ping-pong with my friends. You're not the same mom you used to be."

"Oh. How does that make you feel?"

"I don't like it. This is not who you are."

"Do you think it is because I've changed? Or that you're seeing me differently than you used to?"

"Maybe both. But I like you the way you used to be."

"Hmm. Sometimes I like the way you used to be. I miss holding you and rocking you back and forth and reading you stories. But I don't miss changing your diapers."

"Mom." Of course, he was irritated with me.

"I know. But I think you get the point. I do like you the way you are now."

"That's how it's supposed to be."

"You're right. That *is* how it's supposed to be. Thanks, my son." I reached over to kiss him on the forehead.

A few more check stubs allowed me to refinance our home. It needed a new roof and repairs. I couldn't wait to sell it and move out. The first thing I did was take down the reminders of death over the stone fireplace. I wrapped those three deer heads and stored them in the attic. I transformed that dark-paneled den with a coat of light peach paint.

When my son walked into the house, he burst out in anger. "I can't believe you did this without asking me first." Richard showed up in my son's body!

I talked with my counselor friend about it. "Lisa, what do you think? This has been his home for nineteen years. Should I have asked him first? Isn't it okay for me to paint the den without getting his approval?"

She said something like this: "Oh my gosh, Judy. You're the parent. This is massive change for him. But as a young adult, it won't be long before he leaves to establish his own home. The transition has been more than difficult for all of you."

"Oh, so it's okay for me to be assertive with him? That I'm the one to make final decisions?"

"Yes. And I wonder if he sees himself as the man of the house. He's angry. This is your home, and you need to do what's best to move forward for them and you. Your son will need to process through his emotions. You can't do this for him."

"Thank you, Lisa. I needed to hear that." I held back tears and changed the subject to my new hobby of dancing.

Just as I felt satisfied with the new look in the den, a water pipe had busted in the laundry room. My plumber-neighbor came to my rescue and fixed the pipe. I also had a hole in the ceiling sheetrock the size of a laundry basket. I measured the area, went to the hardware store, and bought supplies for my do-it-yourself project.

With sheetrock dust in my eyes and strained neck, I balanced my weight between the washer and dryer. My built-up frustration exploded into anger, tears, and feeling sorry for myself. It was a hole I couldn't repair. How was I going to get out of this house? How could Richard abandon me for so many years? How could he let this house get so run-down and leave me to fix it? How could he let our marriage and our children and me get so run-down? I couldn't fix it anymore. I couldn't try anymore. It was too much. I couldn't be the superglue that held my family together.

My throat swelled up and a heaving flood of tears burst through. And that was something my plumber-neighbor couldn't fix. I cried until there were no more tears.

I held my family in prayer for years. Who was praying for me? Then I remembered a song I used to sing while strumming my guitar. "It's me, O Lord, standing in the need of prayer." I remembered playing worship tunes on my piano to calm my soul.

My struggles hid under the sheetrock of my life. The pipes burst. I had two master's degrees and now a counseling practice. Yet my children didn't have resources for their degrees. Other parents sacrificed for their kids' education. Mine were left to figure out life on their own. They felt sorry for their dad and were irritated with me. Sometimes their anger showed up out loud. But most of the time it was an undercurrent, just like that pipe.

I had a hard time saying no to them. One time my daughter expected me to dog-sit for her and her friend's dog. As soon as I smelled poop and pee on the carpet, those little mutts ran for cover. I was furious! I grabbed their leashes, but they hid. So I opened the door a crack, and they ran under my feet and out of the house. If they got run over, I didn't care. For months I fought depression. I soaked up guilt while trying to make things right for everyone else.

In a session with Penny, I teared up and said, "I can't do this on my own."

"Judy, you're not alone. You've surrounded yourself with support. You'll need to learn how to say no to your children. Don't try to do for others what only they can do for themselves. I want to remind you that you have what it takes to move through these dark times. And relationships will change."

"Our task is to 'forgive and remember,' then let it go. When we're not forgiven by another, we can still forgive ourselves... We need to remember well enough to glean life lessons from our regrets."

One of my first clients in my new counseling practice was a young adult. "You're not my first counselor," she said from my couch while I followed intake questions and listened to her reasons for coming.

"Oh? Tell me more."

The volume in her energetic voice increased. "I'm SO angry with my parents. I thought everything was fine. Then in my last semester of college Mom called to tell me she and dad were getting divorced. I couldn't sleep, let alone concentrate enough to study."

"Oh, I'm so sorry. What's happened since that time?"

"She's always criticized my dad. And he's so laid back. He complains to me about her. She complains to me about him. I wish they'd leave me alone and let me live my life. I'm so angry I can't stand it."

I couldn't help but imagine what my own daughters were going through. As a newly licensed counselor, I was well aware of transference issues. That's when a client triggers a personal issue in the counselor. In this case, this client triggered my mother/daughter relationships. My self-awareness was crucial here. I needed to show up authentically as her counselor and a human being who was also a mother whose daughters struggled with their parents' divorce. In this case and in several sessions following, my personal disclosure was therapeutic for her. And it helped her to know that her story touched me.

Each client is a divine appointment. Their courage and resilience keep me aware and intentional. I'm there to validate their experiences and come alongside them in their journey. Dr. Benner showed me how to do that.

A male client approaching his forties struggled with social anxiety. "My mom and dad hate each other," he said. "She's always been there for me. Dad wasn't. My mom was the one to meet with my teachers. She confronted them when I wasn't treated like the rest of the class."

"Oh. How do you think I can be of help at this point?"

"I get so angry, and I have a hard time focusing. I've lost jobs and have no confidence. I need my mom, but her health is bad. I moved back home. Dad is mad at me for making his office my bedroom."

I didn't want my sons to struggle with overdependence on me. One of my coworkers was a bitter divorced woman whose adult son lived with her. She was critical of him and men in general. But I wanted to allow my sons to be healthy men in tune with their masculine hearts as I learned from John Eldridge. And I needed to trust my own heart and the female hearts of my daughters. I was aware and intentional to affirm my four, whose hearts I cherished. I reminded them, "You have what it takes to grow into adulthood."

I encouraged my young adult male and female clients to believe that they have what it takes. Some learned the dance of resilience with the steps of growth.

My confidence increased as a counselor when I saw transformations in my clients. With every story, I became aware of the bigger picture of their value and worthiness as human beings deeply loved by God.

Maybe my four would let go of their judgment of me. They would know the story and choose what kind of husbands and wives and moms and dads they'd become. They needed for me to believe in them. I couldn't parent like they were children. I wanted to let them know they have what it takes to launch into the adult life God designed for them.

This wasn't easy; I clung tight. I had nurtured their little newborn bodies close to mine. I gave them life and guidance in the midst of a troubled marriage. I avoided being like the moms of my clients. I became aware of divided loyalties. My four had decisions of their own. And I chose to model growth while intentional prayers filled my journals.

Chapter 19

RISK OF IMAGO

Twenty years from now you will be more disappointed
by the things you didn't do than by the ones you did.
—Mark Twain

B eyond our family of origins, we enter relationships because
our learned dances match another's. Romance is influenced
by neurochemical cocktails designed to boost attachment and
reproduction. The feel-good chemicals are not only short lived, but they
also make us unaware of the potential horsemen. This mixture stimulates
romantic love. Those four chemicals are dopamine, serotonin, oxytocin,
and endorphin. Here's a simple explanation that makes us certain we've
found "the one."

Dopamine anticipates that our needs will be met.

Serotonin is triggered by admiration and pursuit of love.

Oxytocin is released by both sexual and nonsexual physical touch.

Endorphin is stimulated by pain with expectations of comfort.

I read Harville Hendrix's book *Getting the Love You Want*[63] to gain insight about my troubled marriage. Hendrix and his wife, Helen LaKelly Hunt, developed a counseling model that made sense to me. Imago Relationship Therapy[64] helps couples make the space between them emotionally safe using a dialogue method. *Imago* is a Latin term meaning image. We create a positive image of our romantic partner and expect them to heal us from painful experiences of the past. After time when they bust through the illusion of our positive image of them, they become reminders of those who've harmed us. Then we create negative images. Both positive and negative images are familiar in our family of origins. Our creation of them in our partner keeps us unaware. We miss out on our authentic journey while hanging onto fantasies of bliss and despair.

We inadvertently rewound our partner when we defend ourselves. Those defenses (which I've termed as dances) are weapons against the other. We don't realize how we're inviting our partner to feel accused or attacked. In turn, they defend themselves. When the accusation/defensiveness dance escalates, we create wedges of distance. The Stonewall and Contempt horsemen deplete those feel-good neurochemicals. Imago therapy helps couples become aware and intentional to grow beyond messy relationships.

I quit my crisis job within a year and my counseling practice became full-time income. I received an invitation from Ron, a certified Imago therapist who provided weekend intensives called "Getting the Love You

---

63   Harville Hendrix, Ph.D. and Helen LaKelly Hunt, Ph.D. *Getting The Love You Want* (New York: Henry Holt and Company, 2008). More about this amazing couple, their books, trainings, and resources can be found at https://harvilleandhelen.com.

64   Imago Relationship Therapy: http://imagorelationships.org.

Want."[65] Named after the book, the weekend is a trademark of Imago therapy led by highly trained counselors around the world.

Ron offered room and board at a retreat center in exchange for my time and skills to volunteer. Although eager for direct experience with this model, I questioned my ability to help couples since I was divorced. But just as I had intentionally leaned into the story of the abortion, I wanted to understand my troubled marriage. Before saying yes, I asked myself these questions:

What are my intentions?
Can I put myself aside and be present for the couples?
What was my part of the troubled marriage?
Can the weekend experience help me be more aware?

The mountaintop retreat campus reminded me of what I imagined before. This one had arched breezeway entries and patios attached to buildings with clay tile rooflines. It didn't compare to the Byzantine convent. But I still identified with Maria seeking wisdom from the mother nun.

Ron and I met for supper before the couples arrived. "Thanks for asking me to assist," I said. "I'm eager to see this in action since I've read Hendrix's book."

"I'm glad to have you, Judy. These weekends are highlights of my counseling." As a licensed pastoral counselor and Episcopal priest, Ron told me about his couples-only practice. He gave clear directions for how I was to help.

"Just to let you know, I'm freshly divorced as of a few weeks ago. I'm trying to figure out my niche as a counselor."

---

65 Here's where you can find out about the weekend intensives: http://
imagorelationships.org/pub/find-a-workshop/getting-the-love-you-want-couples-
weekend-workshop/.

"Thanks for sharing that with me."

"It was twenty-nine years. But the marriage was comatose for the last decade." I hoped he thought I had a "biblical" divorce. "I wonder if this experience will be like the Retrouvaille weekend my ex-husband and I went to."

"I'm not familiar with Retrouvaille. But the reason I got into this work is part of my story." Ron shared about his first marriage ending in divorce. When he told me that, I became more aware. Like the older couple on the plane, I assumed couples' therapists had solid long-term marriages.

"Both positive and negative images are familiar in our family of origins. Our creation of them in our partner keeps us unaware. We miss out on our authentic journey while hanging onto fantasies of bliss and despair."

The weekend combined learning and experiential exercises. Ron's teaching about "exits" clicked for me. Exits are any activities or energies away from the union. The most catastrophic exits are death or divorce. Others are emotional or sexual affairs. But socially acceptable exits are overwork, church activities, and even homeschooling children. Mental or physical illness can be exits because of hyperfocus on care for the individual, rather than the relationship.

Seasonal exits like starting a business, birthing babies, or caring for an ill spouse are to be expected. But when exits in several areas become chronic, it's likely we're avoiding intimacy in our marriages. No wonder mine didn't last. Yet, when we're aware of exits, we can become intentional about closing the gaps. Couples can learn creative ways to increase the feel-good neurochemicals that connected them in the first place. What a way to learn the resilience/growth dances!

I greeted each couple with a smile at the registration table. "I'm glad to meet you." And I handed them their name tags. Some didn't smile back. I wondered if they were as despondent as I was on that first night of Retrouvaille. I felt tension fill up the room. But I was the "expert" counselor this time. Yet they were more than names crossed off the list. I could only imagine their painful stories. Each couple seemed to fit each other in their physical appearances. But that's what the deacon from the benevolence committee thought of me and Richard.

I sat in the back to be aware and intentional to meet needs. How would the weekend unfold in real life? Was my reading Hendrix's book and his insight about relationships only an ideal? Or did the concepts really work? Maybe this experience would keep me out of a romantic relationship. Or maybe I'd see others making their marriage a honeymoon like the older couple I met on the plane.

The mixture of teaching, guided meditations, and group activities helped spouses increase compassion and empathy toward each other. Ron used a volunteer couple to demonstrate the holding exercise. One spouse held the other like a newborn baby. They looked into each other's eyes while soft music played. Then they switched places so both could experience holding the other. Then all the couples in the room held each other.

Another activity was like a version of musical chairs. To prepare, each person wrote a list of what they admired about their spouse. It included characteristics, behaviors, and traits. One partner (times a roomful) sat in a chair while the other circled around whispering

> "*Imago* is a Latin term meaning image. We create a positive image of our romantic partner and expect them to heal us from painful experiences of the past."

positive characteristics from the list. Volume increased to the next level while the same spouse verbalized positive behaviors. The next notch up of music volume invited louder voices. Each spouse circled the other with positive traits. Highest volume music cued shouts of global phrases. "YOU'RE WONDERFUL" or "YOU'RE AMAZING" or "YOU'RE AWESOME AND I'M SO LUCKY TO BE MARRIED TO YOU." It sounded like parents cheering their player's home run! I watched as if I sat with a textbook and yellow highlighter on metal bleachers. Tense faces had turned to laughter and tears. All those couples together reminded me of my brief encounter with the older couple on the plane.

That room full of feel-good chemicals was contagious. I signed up to participate in a therapist-only weekend for singles called "Keeping the Love You Find."[66] I arrived at a different retreat center and joined a circle of counselors much like my first spiritual direction group retreat. Jane, the facilitator/Imago therapist, modeled transparency, inviting all of us to enter our authentic journeys. She shared her story of being freshly divorced. But it was her second one. How could she have such wisdom and be twice divorced? I felt compassion and determined not to make the same mistakes. The more aware and intentional I became, the less likely I would repeat my dances in a second marriage. I was thankful to be single. And I appreciated Jane's courage to be her authentic self.

My status as a divorced therapist was no longer a hindrance to my couples counseling. And I asked myself and others, would Imago therapy be the right direction for me? I was still new to private practice. It would be a risk because of the huge commitment of time and money. But I could include the program as continuing education hours required to maintain my state licensure and national certification. I applied and decided Imago therapy would become my specialty. It would improve

---

66   Find out more about the Keeping the Love You Find Workshop: http://
     imagorelationships.org/pub/find-a-workshop/keeping-the-love-you-find/.

my personal relationships and bring more healing from divorce. I could grow from my automatic dances.

Through my certification training I was mentored by a husband/wife team who were both Imago therapists.[67] Wendy and Bob had a solid long-term marriage and had raised a grown son and daughter. For a total of twelve days at three different intervals within the year, I sat in a circle of trusted peer therapists. We became mirrors to each other through dialogue and role play. We honored our vulnerable selves through the context of our training. How much more insight could I have gotten with a room full of Imago-trained therapists? We all became more aware of how we created our relationship messes.

I gained awareness from lessons of regrets about my marriage. It inspired me to write a list of things I needed in a significant relationship. And I wrote another list of things I would not tolerate. Those two lists became my guidelines when I would otherwise be blinded by romantic chemistry. As I struggled less with my Baptist doctrine, I experienced real married couples connect beyond my Christian theology. Three decades was too big a chunk of life not to examine my blind spots.

Was there some hidden agenda in my heart that I didn't know about? How could I have saved my marriage? I didn't want to fall into the same dance patterns with a new one. I couldn't get the older couple on the airplane out of my head. I took more deep breaths of AIR in my awareness, intentions, and risks.

And God was showing up for me in both spiritual and secular retreat experiences.

---

67   Find out more about P2 Partnerships at http://relationshipcoaching.net/about-us.

Chapter 20

RISK OF REMARRIAGE

For now we see in a mirror, dimly, but then face-to-face. Now I know in part, but then I shall know just as I also am known.
—1 Corinthians 13:12

We can move toward intentional risks with increased awareness. Yet we'll remain stuck if our intentions don't move us into action. Another Scripture passage uses the analogy of looking in a mirror after becoming aware. This verse references an unstable person.

...he is like a man observing his natural face in a mirror; for he observes himself, goes away, and immediately forgets what kind of man he was.[68]

---

68   James 1:23, 24

Marriage can provide opportunities for self-awareness that's impossible in any other relationship. When we recognize our own flaws (the log in our eyes) rather than hyperfocus on our spouse's (speck in their eyes),[69] we can be intentional to appreciate their showing us our path to growth.

They, as well as we, are distorted mirrors to each other. Some of us are convex or concave mirrors, like the ones at an amusement park. Others of us may be flatter mirrors for more accurate reflections that honor our dignity, worthiness, and lovability. God's perfect flat mirror can help us consider our partner's viewpoints as divine invitations.

We also have mirror neurons in our brains.[70] Just as the feel-good chemicals were contagious in the room full of couples, our brain chemistry changes in the presence of others. Our mirror neurons trigger reciprocal interactions in relationships. When we smile at babies, they smile back at us. When others are kind to us, we're kind to them. If we think negative thoughts without verbalizing, the mirror neurons of others sense the tension. Of course, we can't read each other's minds. But we can be aware of how mirror neurons pick up "metacommunications." Nonverbal messages include body language, muscle tension in the face, gestures, and even dilation in our eyes.

> "Just as the feel-good chemicals were contagious in the room full of couples, our brain chemistry changes in the presence of others. Our mirror neurons trigger reciprocal interactions in relationships."

Even though our spouse reflects from a flawed mirror, they still give us the gift of awareness. We can grow our character and know our blind spots through the mirrors of our relationships.

---

69   The contrast of the log and speck in the eyes is taken from Matthew 7:3, New American Standard Bible.

70   This is a scholarly article about mirror neurons: https://www.ncbi.nlm.nih.gov/pmc/articles/PMC5810456/.

———————

Joe and I enjoyed hikes, bike rides, and canoe trips. He respected my symbolic dancing as meeting God in the movement and rhythm of life. We went to more dance parties than I ever did in high school. And I had more fun than I ever imagined in college. We attended his Catholic Masses and my Baptist Sunday school classes while unaware of our romantic chemistry.

I presented workshops about forgiveness, and Joe edited technical parts of my PowerPoints. He "got me," and we connected spiritually. One day during a hike at the nature center he shared stories of his bipolar episodes.

"I caused my parents a lot of grief when I had my first episode at nineteen. I rode my bike in the rain and collapsed on the living room floor. I woke up in the emergency room with police and tech workers yelling at me. They drugged me to the point I couldn't even speak. No one knew my diagnosis then."

"Oh, wow. I'm sorry you went through all that."

"It wasn't until I turned forty that I finally got on the right medication. My last episode happened a decade ago. I hooked up my camper and took my dog, Pup, to get away from the stress. I was totally off medication. But within three weeks I went to my psychiatrist's office and got my prescription. I didn't go to the hospital then and continued on with life as normal." I was fascinated with Joe's stories of endurance.

I still struggled at home dealing with post-divorce anger. I was left with the decision to euthanize our Labrador retriever. My son's car accident left him with depression that outlasted his temporary disability in a wheelchair. With every stressful incident, I soaked up blame, feeling faithless and insecure. In one of my prayers, I wrote:

Help me be the loving mom my sons and daughters need. Please multiply my prayers. Powerfully break through the feebleness of my faith.

How could I exchange my leftover mourning for dancing? Grief and anger cycled through me again and again. The aftermath of divorce left me feeling responsible for the well-being of four others, even though the girls had moved out, and one moved back in. But I was growing weary as a single parent of adolescents.

One day at my office I received a text from my oldest, now a young adult. My three o'clock appointment had canceled, and soon my daughter sat on the couch of my sacred space with tears in her eyes. I sat close, ready to hear her apology about causing me frustration over the dog-sitting incident. Instead she said, "Mom, you're going to be a grandmother…"

Tears mixed with our embrace. "Oh, I'm so happy. How do you feel about it?" My response would forever be etched in her history.

"I'm happy and scared." I listened more.

That evening I took her and my future son-in-law out to dinner since we didn't know each other well. Months later, my first granddaughter was born along with a dimension of love I couldn't explain. I entered the grandparent club with a new name, "Mimi."

My friendship with Joe endured family transitions and traumas. But my becoming a grandmother opened more layers for us to question our future direction. So we attended a few couples counseling sessions with his therapist and my therapist. Could the challenges of his bipolar disorder handle a romance? And I reviewed the two lists from my Imago weekend.

One evening close to my birthday, Joe and I were dance hosts at a special event with a live band at Rock City on Lookout Mountain.[71] While others mingled after dinner, we took a stroll to Lover's Leap in the cool night air holding hands. While looking at the stars above and lights in the valley below, we rested from our synchronized swing dances. As we stood on Lover's Leap, Joe gave me what I thought was a birthday gift.

"What's this?"

"Oh, something."

"How do I open it?" The geometrically shaped wooden box with a slick shine was a rare find at an antique store. "What is this?" I said. We laughed through my struggle since I couldn't figure out how to open it.

"This is so funny. She can't open it," Joe said. Through our giggles I didn't notice another watching. "Here, let me help you."

"No, I've got it. Let me try." With our playful tug-of-war, I heard someone else laughing. When I opened the box, a bright light shone. "Oh my gosh. What's this?"

He rigged a miniature light to make it beam out of the box.

"What's this?" I asked again.

"Just look."

"Oh my gosh. It's a ring!" I took out the diamond ring and held it up. "What does this mean?"

He forgot to answer and just laughed. His friend rolled the video camera. We smiled and hugged when I realized it was an engagement ring. It fit my left ring finger perfectly. In my excitement I still asked, "What do I tell the children? And what does this really mean?"

Still concerned about pleasing all four, I wondered if it was even possible. Would our efforts to please create more stress? Could I take that risk of faith and let go of trying?

---

71 You can see pictures of Lover's Leap through Rock City's website: http://www.seerockcity.com.

My youngest still believed the theology in which he was raised. *Whoever divorces… And marries another commits adultery.*[72] But he was too young to struggle with his beliefs as I had. And I had a hard time explaining my "biblical divorce" without dishonoring his dad. I wanted the attention to be on my daughter's wedding since they decided to birth before saying "I do." She needed the freedom to recreate the wedding of her imagination and be a fairy-tale bride.

My home needed to be sold, and Joe had the skills to do it. Our solid friendship and slow-growing romance made marriage the next right step. My list of "pros and cons" along with his persuasive steps was our dance into saying "I do." I avoided the attention of being a new bride so we could naturally move into our marriage just as we naturally moved on the dance floor.

It was a risk. One son had already moved in with his dad. Joe and I getting married would force the other son into his adulthood. He eventually rented a house with two roommates. And we decided on a private wedding on the shores of Lake Michigan. Then we gathered with extended family who supported us on my grandmother's ninetieth birthday.

"Marriage can provide opportunities for self-awareness that's impossible in any other relationship."

---

72   Matthew 19:19. Rachel Held Evans (who also graduated from the same conservative Christian college as I did) challenges our thinking about a "biblical marriage," which includes a woman being forced to marry her rapist; *A Year of Biblical Womanhood* (Nashville: Thomas Nelson, 2012). Also, David Instone-Brewer, in his book *Divorce and Remarriage in the Church: Biblical Solutions for Pastoral Realities* (InterVarsity Press, 2003), is a book for those struggling with "biblical divorce" theology.

Along with new marriage adjustments, we expected tension from living in the home that bore years of my family's memories. Grief and sadness mixed with our new beginnings and my needing to let go of "normal alignments," especially with my sons. But it was so hard.

My new husband sat across from me on the back porch after cleaning out the attic. The remaining boxes were filled with trophies of the boys' baseball tournaments. Joe never had children of his own, but empathy flowed through his tears. We wept together in his grief for me and compassion for Richard. Joe's capacity to feel and love me so deeply was the partnership I dreamed of.

Both sons came over to pick up their memories. We all needed to say goodbye to their boyhoods. And I needed to let them be men. It wasn't easy, but I knew it was good and right.

Joe transformed our home, my memories, and my life as a woman deeply cherished. Of course, we experienced normal stress in our first year as husband and wife. Yet, he met every criterion on the list I made years before of what I needed to be loved and cared for.

He fixed the ceiling in the laundry room, trimmed every pink azalea bush, and sculpted the overarching banana magnolia tree. He pressure-washed the stone walkway, making it look brand new. From the smallest nail holes to the fist-sized damage, he patched and smoothed all sheetrock walls. He touched up and repainted over the light peach color I had changed from the darkly paneled den. He detailed every baseboard and trim and replaced bathroom counters and sinks. We decluttered, simplified, and took family pictures off the walls to aid the imaginations of potential buyers. It was a move-in-ready dollhouse and sold quickly after the finished projects.

Joe was my hero as we left the old home to begin new memories. He was my soul mate, my dance partner, and my loyal husband. Just as the couple on the plane gave me a vision of marriage, I imagined our new home.

During a counseling session at my office, a female client shared her memories. "The happiest moments of my childhood were when I visited my grandparents. My grandmother listened to me and made me feel special. I could tell her anything. I loved being at that old farmhouse." The stress fell along with tears down her face as she reflected on her younger self. Her story drove me to envision a home that would build memories for my future grandchildren.

Tension from projects on the old house transferred to our "Mimi" home that needed just as much remodeling. Joe worked his magic. He knocked out a large paneled wall between the kitchen and living room, making the 1970s personality transform to an open retreat-like home. Nestled on our wooded acre lot at the foot of Lookout Mountain, our trilevel became my vision come true. We hosted pool parties in the summer and dances on our great room wood floor in the winter. Laughter, relationships, movement, and hope filled every space.

Powder-white snow showed up for our first Christmas like the nostalgia of a Norman Rockwell painting.[73] My sons and daughters along with their families lit the advent candle next to the crackling fire in the stone fireplace. From the youngest to the oldest, we opened presents around the tree and felt the warmth while looking through the snow globe of our floor-length windows.

Joe won the hearts of my sons and daughters, some of whom had become parents and spouses. The grandchildren loved visits and playtime on the tire swing "Papi Joe" made for them. Our marriage was solid, and our home was a peaceful place to relax after a full day of counseling.

I put away my blue leather Bible with my old name engraved along with highlights and tear-crumpled pages. My new, clean Bible would hold fresh highlights of passages that jumped off the page and into my heart. I felt new intimacy in my relationship with Christ, and I loved the

---

73 For more nostalgia, there's even a Norman Rockwell Museum: https://store.nrm. org.

spiritual bond in my marriage as we swayed to the rhythm of worship. I was less desperate—centered and more thankful in my prayer journals.

Chapter 21

RISK OF BIPOLAR

One does not discover new lands without consenting
to lose sight of the shore for a very long time.
—André Gide

Θhe *Diagnostic and Statistical Manual of Mental Disorders*[74] is like the Bible for mental health professionals. It's used to diagnose and treat individuals. Nonmedical professionals such as licensed counselors, social workers, and psychologists treat through talk therapy, mindfulness, or a multitude of other modalities. Medical professionals include psychiatrists and nurse practitioners who treat through prescribing psychotropic medications. Some also provide talk therapy along with their services.

---

74 At the time of this writing, the DSM-V is the current edition. You can find out more from the American Psychiatric Association website: https://www.psychiatry. org/psychiatrists/practice/dsm.

Symptoms alone are not cause for concern unless they cluster in severity, interfering with functioning at home or work. And every person who has a diagnosis of any kind is not that illness. One of my pet peeves is when I hear the phrase "he's bipolar" or "she's bipolar." The "he" or "she" is not bipolar. Rather, they are persons of value and dignity just like any other human being with or without a disorder attached. We don't say "he's depression" or "she's anxiety."

We must break through the stigma of mental health by being aware of our language around it. Jessica Knowles,[75] an actress, writer, singer, and director, gives us insight into her bipolar diagnosis. She challenges us to use the term "mental differences"[76] in place of "mental illness."

With my diagnosis of ADHD (attention deficit hyperactivity disorder),[77] I've become aware of how it has affected my marriages. In her book *The ADHD Effect on Marriage*, Melissa Orlov[78] helps us understand symptoms of the diagnosis and how common messes emerge between spouses when one or both have ADHD. Increased awareness through reading this book helps us recognize many symptoms from my story. To name a few, they include:

- Difficulty organizing
- Easily distracted

---

75 You can find Jessica Knowles on Facebook at https://www.facebook.com/jessie. knowles1.

76 Although I first heard this term from Jessica, she later told me it originated with Petra Kuppers. It has been a pattern since the 1900s to change terms to avoid stigma for those with "mental differences." This website from Great Britain provides us a perspective: http://broughttolife.sciencemuseum.org.uk/ broughttolife/themes/mentalhealthandillness.

77 The DSM-IV differentiated ADHD from ADD, listing symptoms for children. The current DSM-V dropped the other variations. The official diagnosis is attention deficit hyperactivity disorder. Overall, the DSM-V takes into account developmental stages with all diagnostic categories.

78 Melissa Orlov, *The ADHD Effect on Marriage* (Plantation, FL: Specialty Press), 2010. For more resources go to: https://www.addrc.org/the-adhd-effect-on-marriage/.

- Loses things necessary for tasks
- Many projects going on simultaneously
- Intolerance of boredom
- Impulsivity
- Search for high stimulation

It's important to note that ADHD symptoms are similar to the symptoms of bipolar disorder. And to simplify a complex description, bipolar moods range from mild to severe in three major categories: Cyclothymia, Bipolar II, and Bipolar I. A hypomanic high that lasts more than four days might compare with the excitement we feel watching live from the stands our favorite team win the Super Bowl. A manic episode lasts longer than a week. Using our same example, it might feel like we're the quarterback of the winning Super Bowl team! Depressive episodes for all three categories range with intensity from minor irritability to severe suicidal ideation. Manic and hypomanic symptoms include:

- Grandiosity
- Decreased need for sleep
- Pressured speech
- Distractibility
- Flight of ideas
- Increase in goal-directed activities
- Excessive pleasurable risks with potential for painful consequences

---

I didn't know what this new role of husband felt like inside Joe's head. His history and pattern of self-care made him my hero. Having always been a single man, we expected our beginnings to be challenging. He'd share his life with a relationship therapist and professional counselor. He

"One of my pet peeves is when I hear the phrase 'he's bipolar' or 'she's bipolar.' The 'he' or 'she' is not bipolar. Rather, they are persons of value and dignity just like any other human being with or without a disorder attached."

laughed along with my teasing when he told others about his bipolar disorder. I'd say, "And he didn't used to be my client. We met through ballroom dancing."

Others smiled and said things like, "Ballroom dancing! I wish my husband would dance with me." Or they'd say, "How romantic!"

As we adjusted to married life, he held me in bed until I went to sleep. Then he went to his "man cave" to do his thinking and research. His energy normally reached its peak at midnight and beyond. Many times he'd be in the garage working on a project, or welding something, or refinishing furniture.

I'd never seen him sick or witnessed his manic episodes. But I became aware of his daily struggles to live with intense emotions. Normal stressors could be difficult.

Joe's hypersensitivity helped me to be a more self-aware counselor, wife, and mother. My intensity could easily offend certain clients. And some of my relationship "issues" with Joe were similar to how my sons and daughters experienced me. I was conscious of my facial expressions and tone of voice. I worked on being more understanding and empathic. Joe and I became more connected beyond our conflicts. We could be partners beyond the dance floor.

He agreed to attend marriage conferences and enrichment weekends to grow our relationship. We'd been to several in our first four years. Marriage Encounter[79] was a mild version of Retrouvaille. We learned techniques to identify our feelings through letter writing. We came back determined to write regular love letters to each other with a method simple enough for nonwriters. We described our emotions with

---

79 Website for Marriage Encounter: http://www.wwme.org.

intentional connection. The couples we met there showed us steps to the listen/understand dance. They were versions of David and Juliet Benner.

With Joe's research mentality, we shopped online and visited bookstores. We compared, touched, sized, and smelled dozens of blank books ranging from leather to spiral bound. We picked two matching brown hardback journals. They were plain and elegant enough to express our love. Their pages were acid-free with gold edges. One was for him to write letters to me. And the other was for me to write letters to him.

A few weeks later as we sat on the front porch, Joe said, "I don't want to do this anymore. I've never been a good writer."

"It's not the grammar or quality that matters. Remember how close we felt to each other on the weekend?"

"Yes. And I think we still can. But this just doesn't work for me."

Since I was on the verge of nagging, I backed off. Although it was a familiar disappointment, I wrote to him in my journal on special days. Generally, when we give greeting cards to those we love, after a time those cards end up in the trash. But, my words would last in the blank books we carefully chose together.

We attended another weekend at the same Jesuit retreat center where I met Dr. Benner for spiritual direction. And yet another weekend was called "Passionate Intimacy" led by sex therapists and a conference room of a hundred other couples.[80] All those weekends increased my confidence in Joe as my husband and bonded us in our new marriage.

Even though some dances from the old marriage showed up in the new, Joe was a different man. I kept writing in my journal with occasional visits to Penny, my therapist. I practiced Imago concepts to help calm our reactions with each other.

One of our dance dates was at the weekly party at our instructor's studio. Joe was Linda's favorite male student, and she asked him a favor.

---

80   Website for Passionate Intimacy program: https://intimatemarriage.org.

"Joe, do you have any plans two Saturdays from now? I'd like to use you for my teaching partner at the dance workshop."

"As far as I know, I don't have anything going on," he said. And he pulled out his calendar to mark the date.

As I overheard the conversation, I interrupted. "What time on Saturday will this be? Remember this is the day of my daughter's wedding. I can't believe you forgot!"

"Oh, well never mind," Linda said with a lighthearted tone. "It's no problem at all."

But Joe stopped abruptly and gave me a harsh look.

"I'm sorry, I just wanted to remind you before you made a commitment," I said. When his glare didn't change, I walked away leaving him standing with Linda. We were the newlyweds among our friends. After that neither of us felt like dancing. We changed out of our dance shoes and left.

In the parking lot, I said, "What just happened?"

"You need to think ahead of time before confronting me like that. Then you walked away."

"Oh my gosh. I didn't mean to 'confront' you. I walked away because I felt humiliated."

"You embarrassed me in front of Linda."

"What? Are you serious?"

Silent tension remained after the drive home. He pulled away when I tried reaching out with gentle touches. Could he only see me through the irritable lens of his bipolar disorder? Is that why he accused me of being reactive? The next day I wrote him a letter in a different journal. The other was saved for special days and events.

I'm saddened that my heart is so misunderstood by you. I long for the same respect that I give you. It's a pattern for me to put myself

aside and sit and listen to you and get into your world. I experience
invalidation and harsh judgment from you. You react angrily when
I ask simple questions. I don't deserve that. I'm wondering if this is
what I'm required to "deal with" due to your mood swings? How do
you balance tolerance with bipolar disorder? Where does personal
responsibility come in when moods get out of line?

After a restful sleep, Joe softened his heart and listened to my concerns. He apologized. Our yearly marriage enrichment weekends were a safety net for us. We continued occasional couples counseling. Fun times of camping, dancing, and bike riding balanced us beyond the irritable times. After all, we lived in that old home our first year. Things would be different now that we'd settled into a more peaceful environment, a comfortable home that would minimize his mood triggers.

Each argument reminded me of the old marriage and the pain of losing my children's loyalty. I tried being less cluttered even though my ADHD made it a lifelong challenge. I tiptoed in the mornings to avoid waking him up from his light sleeping. Even though I was the "expert" about relationships, I didn't take continuing education classes to learn more about bipolar disorder, or ADHD.

Our grandchildren's weekend visits were my vision come true. We were "Mimi" and "Papi Joe." He surprised the children with tractor rides, bonfires, and tire swings. One New Year's Eve, he bought sparkling grape juice, hats, and shakers. He rigged up a projector that showed patterns of colorful lights on the walls that danced to the music. Through our internet, he found a live-streaming program of Great Britain's celebration. We counted down to the New Year with Big Ben striking twelve at seven o'clock local time. The children danced after midnight until their bedtime at nine o'clock local time.

Joe was great at grocery shopping, preparing healthy meals, and doing house chores. He made sure I came home to an orderly and peaceful place to relax each day.

It was four and a half years into the marriage when I picked up the brown hardback journal. I wrote a Valentine and added red hearts with colored pencils.

Thank you for being my Valentine! I appreciate even more that we are soul mates and best friends particularly in these precious years of our lives when life is still full and energetic and adventurous!

But that's when I missed the signs.

Chapter 22
RISKIER RISKS

Only those who will risk going too far can
possibly find out how far it is possible to go.
—T. S. Eliot

According to research, mild-mannered couples are no more or less healthy than high-intensity couples. But what does matter is how quickly they recover from "ruptures" when they occur. Reptilian reactions are inevitable in our marriages; remember that 69 percent of conflict in our relationships is perpetual, without resolve, even in healthy and growing marriages. But getting back into partnership without irrevocable damage is the key.

And, in a perfect world, we'd want our partnerships to grow into more connection beyond every conflict. Forgiveness, reconciliation, and resilience are variable attributes with every couple.

Also, stereotypical roles and expectations emerge through the messes. For example, in about one in four marriages, the wife earns more than her husband.[81] That same ratio applies to couples choosing to sleep in separate bedrooms.[82] Many homes are built with two master suites. Separate bedrooms are ways some spouses minimize the Four Horsemen. When both husband and wife sleep well, it decreases irritations and grumpy attitudes. Rob and Laura, the couple played by Dick Van Dyke and Mary Tyler Moore, may have been ahead of their time with the twin bed scenes in the 1960s sitcom.[83]

"Reptilian reactions are inevitable in our marriages ... getting back into partnership without irrevocable damage is the key ... Forgiveness, reconciliation, and resilience are variable attributes with every couple."

Sleep is one of the first things I assess in treating individuals and couples struggling with depression or anxiety. Lack of sleep is even more foundational to our well-being than exercise and proper nutrition, although all three are basics to our quality of life. Most adults need seven to eight hours of sleep each evening. Lack of quality sleep causes

---

81   2018 United States Census Bureau study reports on the estimated 25 percent of wives earning more than their husbands, https://www.census.gov/content/dam/Census/library/working-papers/2018/demo/SEHSD-WP2018-20.pdf.

82   A National Institute of Health 2005 survey indicates 25 percent of married couples sleep separately, https://sleepfoundation.org/sites/default/files/subscription/sub003.txt.

83   Rob and Laura's dream marriage is captured in this short video that includes a kiss in one of their twin beds of their master bedroom: https://www.youtube.com/watch?v=jeLTAtOJA7Q.

weight gain, more stress, and less focus. Plus, it's the number one factor underlying mental illness.

I encourage clients to stay away from their screens an hour before bed. The blue light affects our circadian rhythms and melatonin, which regulate our sleep patterns. Regular bedtime routines along with waking up at the same time each day could make a huge difference in improving mental health issues and marital messes.

With Joe's disability our nontraditional roles made me the primary breadwinner. Along with caring for our home, he facilitated weekly bipolar support groups in the community. He made our dollars stretch by researching every major purchase from smartphones to vehicles. And he always thought of new ways to make our lives better.

One of my counseling couples that like to go camping said to me, "We almost got a divorce over pop-up camping. We don't do it anymore." They traded their pop-up for a full camper. But I didn't tell them my husband created systems that made our camping easy. That wasn't the time for counselor disclosure.

The system became known as our "Pack N Play." We mounted our seventeen-foot red Mohawk canoe on top with bicycles on the back. Our pop-up camper attached to the trailer hitch. Joe researched destinations with rivers, bike trails, and utility hookups. Our four adventures a year gave us a good work/life balance. It nurtured our marriage beyond the yearly marriage enrichment weekends.

Joe comforted me when I said goodbye to my son who moved to Seattle. He cried along with me as I said goodbye to my daughter and granddaughter who moved to San Diego. He felt along with me when each grandchild was born. And he held me close when I cried for days after my youngest son became a husband.

A clay cup crafted by a potter in Seattle was a Christmas gift from my son Andrew. Its handle formed perfectly to my grip while I sipped the mild-blend coffee from its rim. I began most mornings sitting in the rocking chair on my front porch with a lighted candle, my Bible, prayer journal, and clay cup. The ritual grounded me before facing a full day of clients. The cup made me feel close to Andrew. And it was a tangible connection with the other three.

One day my cup sat on the crowded kitchen countertop along with too much clutter. Gravity was faster than my impulse. In slow motion, it fell. I reached out, but it shattered to the floor. A nauseous pit in my stomach screamed out. Joe picked up the pieces. Then he held me while I cried in his arms.

Earlier in the year, Joe had directed a committee of leaders to organize a Mental Health Awareness event in which he was the master of ceremonies. The local news interviewed him, and he received other opportunities. He attended a training in Washington, DC.

One morning he received a phone call informing him that one of the participants in his support group had died suddenly. Joe told me about his dream of looking into the eyes of someone who died as if he'd had a premonition. We attended the funeral, but Joe became preoccupied with this man's life, his interests, his adventures, and the books he'd written. I was interested too. Of course, this man's bipolar disorder wasn't public knowledge.

Weeks before I said, "It's been over a year since we went to our last marriage weekend. And I've wanted to hear this expert for years. Several people have told me what a difference this conference made in their marriages. I'd like for us to go."

"I don't know," Joe said. "I don't want the pressure right now. I'll let you know later."

I was still skilled at the persuasion dance. "Don't you think it's better to attend a local event than drive hours away? Think of the money and time we'll save."

"We'll talk about it later."

I was used to his irritability. So, I intended to ask again in a couple of days. He'd become more patient if we experienced the conference together, I thought.

About a week later I said, "I understand if you don't want to go. But I'm going. It will help me be familiar with it in case I want to refer couples."

"Do you want me to go?" he asked.

"Yes. That would be better."

"I don't know how we can do it. I told you I'd be speaking to a group of therapists on Saturday afternoon about the support group."

"Oh, I know. I thought we could drive separately. We can catch Friday night's session. Then you can drive home in time to speak on Saturday."

He agreed, but I was unaware he hadn't slept well. He always went to bed after me.

That Friday was the day I settled into the hotel room and got the strange call from the bondsman. When I drove into the jail parking lot, my son's name showed up on my smartphone. I never refuse calls from my children unless I'm with a client or in the bathroom. In between the rings I imagined: "Oh, hi Andrew! How are you, my son? Oh, how am I doing, you ask? You wouldn't believe it, but I just drove into this parking lot, and I'm meeting a bondsman to get Joe out of jail."

I didn't answer. What story would I have for my children, who had learned to trust Joe? There'd better be some kind of explanation. I wasn't putting up with this craziness. I couldn't believe he didn't want to go THAT badly to this conference. If we attended the evening session, the speaker and a room full of husbands would soften his attitude, I reasoned.

I met the bondsman, whom I didn't trust, and gave him money I earned from clients. I signed papers while shaking with anger. I waited for the police officer to get Joe. He collected his wallet and personal items. Knowing I held power between us, with gentleness he said, "Thank you for getting me." And he gave me a hug.

"You'd better have a good explanation for this, Joe. What's going on? And where's the vehicle?"

"I'll explain later. For now, we need to get the car. They impounded it. How much cash do you have?"

"Whoa. Wait a minute. It's after five and they're closed. Let's go on to the session. We can get the car tomorrow."

"Don't you remember? I'm speaking to that group of therapists tomorrow. I need to get it now. I know you wanted to go to the conference, but you need to understand. I've got to get my car tonight."

We missed the Friday session and got back to the hotel room late. After a good night's rest, all would be well. We could recover just as we had in the past. He left the next morning, and I stayed for Saturday's session. I wished Joe could have heard this speaker. His attitude would have changed. But something churned inside me that I ignored.

When I arrived at the front door of our home, he had supper prepared with a lighted candle on the table and soft music playing. This was his way of saying "I'm sorry." Then I saw my daughter's name on my phone. I wasn't going to miss a call this time. "You don't mind if I get this, do you? It won't be long."

"Go ahead," he said. There was no anger or irritation in his voice then.

After a quick FaceTime visit, I said goodbye to my long-distance daughter and granddaughter. Food was on the table, ready for us to settle into the candlelight. I'd hear the real story, and all would make sense. Joe must be in the garage. I went upstairs to change my clothes. Then I went downstairs to let him know I was ready. But he wasn't there. I looked in the driveway, and his car was gone.

It was then I became aware. Something was wrong.

Chapter 23

DANCE OF BLACK AND WHITE

Life isn't about waiting for the storm to pass ...
It's about learning to dance in the rain.
——**Vivian Greene**

S tudents who handwrite their notes in class retain more information from lectures. They test better than laptop users. In the same way, handwriting in a physical blank book is better than keystroking thoughts digitally. The dexterity of using a pen on pages in a journal gives tangible form and clearer insights to reactions and emotions. Author and editor Susan Reynolds says it well. "Handwriting is one of the most advanced human capabilities, because it combines all the complexities of language in concert with intricate psychomotor activity."[84]

84 Susan Reynolds, *Fire Up Your Writing Brain: How to Use Proven Neuroscience to Become a More Creative, Productive, and Successful Writer* (Cincinnati: Writer's Digest Books, 2015), p. 17.

Many of my clients have learned to minimize their anxiety by writing in an "anxiety journal." Rather than dealing with intrusive thoughts, they set a daily appointment for ten minutes or more to honor their worry. By writing at an appointed time, they can close the journal and put it on the shelf or hide it under their mattress for privacy. That gets it out of their heads and onto the page. They're free to focus on things more productive.

Questions to evaluate thoughts
- Are the thoughts true or false?
- If they're true, are they useful to think about now?
- What are the facts?
- What are the stories or meanings we've attached to those facts?

The physical act of writing slows us down enough to gain insight. When we write out prayers and concerns, ruminating thoughts can hold less power. We have the choice to evaluate them objectively. We can make sense of the stories or feelings we have about circumstances we're in.

And if writing in a blank book is too frightening, use paper to be shredded or burned afterwards. The idea is to increase awareness and become intentional—and to get unwanted thoughts out of our heads. Our minds are too precious to invite the temporary guests of our feelings as permanent residents.

Many believe they "can't help thinking" certain thoughts. Yet, when thoughts get stuck in the mind, they make our illusions seem real. Instead of seeing them as distorted images reflected in concave mirrors at an amusement park, we automatically think they're true.

Another analogy I use when I lead guided meditations is this. Imagine thoughts as birds perching on an electrical wire. Breathe in and notice. When breathing out, see the birds fly away. Then become aware of the present moment of the breath. We can keep them from building nests on our heads.

"When we write out prayers and concerns, ruminating thoughts can hold less power. We have the choice to evaluate them objectively."

One of my writing mentors believes that authors who write in the horror genre are emotionally healthier than others.[85] Rather than denying their dark side, they create outlets through their novels. It must be sort of an internal cleansing that makes darkness useful. We can understand why handwriting is so helpful.

It's all in black and white with handwritten words. When I wrote that Valentine's Day love letter, I acknowledged what I thought was a spiritual awakening in Joe. He surrounded himself with accountability groups. And he developed a friendship with a couple much like I had with my spiritual directors. I wrote in my brown hardback journal just two weeks before the jail incident:

Dear Joe, I love your heart of openness to God—and currently your spiritual awakening! I love you for making room for deep substance-

---

85   One of my "writing mentors" includes my listening to several episodes of Joanna Penn's podcast, The Creative Penn.

filled friendships. Your Monday men's group and spiritual direction couple you've been meeting.

When I discovered he was gone, I called our Anglican priest. He and Joe were trusted friends. "Brian, Joe disappeared. Do you know where he is? Has he been acting strange to you?"

"I don't know where he is. But he has been acting different lately."

"Oh? Tell me more. No, not now. Do you know where he could be? Never mind. Can you meet me at the church? He might be there. I don't know where else he'd be."

"Let's start there. I'm leaving now."

I blew out the candles and left food on the table. I grabbed my purse and drove to the church. A live community concert was underway there. Brian waited outside while I went in to look for Joe. It was dark as I shuffled through the crowd. I spotted Joe and inched my way to him. The music was too loud, but our faces were close enough to hear each other.

"What are you doing here?" he asked.

"That's what I was getting ready to ask you. What's going on? I didn't know you left."

"This is not the place to talk."

"I agree. Brian's waiting outside for us. Come join us." I grabbed his sweaty hand while he followed me through the crowd.

"Hey, Joe," Brian said. "Let's go across the street. It's quieter there. Okay?" His cautious manner wasn't their normal interaction. We entered a classroom next to the office. Brian grabbed chairs for us to sit on.

"What's going on, man?" Brian asked. Joe's agitation was too evident.

"Everything's good."

"It doesn't look that way to me."

"Yeah?"

"Yeah, man. You look nervous. Are you?

"Something feels different."

"Judy called me and said you had a nice dinner on the table. Then you left without telling her?"

"Yeah, I just needed to get away. Everything was closing in on me. I had to get outta there."

"What's going on, buddy?"

Then Joe looked at me and said, "Judy, I didn't tell you this before, but the reason I drove so fast yesterday is because they were following me. I had to. When the police pulled me over, they saved my life."

"What? Who's 'they'?"

"It's a conspiracy. The army has been looking for me. They've been trying to find me for a long time. I had to speed. They're after me. They know I have special powers."

"What?" I said. "You've got to be kidding."

"I didn't tell you about this before. But I've been chosen by God. This is my life's purpose. It always has been. I've been trying to figure out how to tell you. But I knew you wouldn't understand."

I played along this time, but my ears throbbed. "Maybe I'll understand." Brian and I made eye contact.

"I didn't want to hurt you, Judy. But we've never been married."

"Oh?"

"I didn't know how you would fit in this plan because I really do love you. But you're not my wife. I've been chosen. I'm married to the Virgin Mary."

"Oh?"

"Yes. It's true. You know we've not had much sex anyway." Suddenly my face got warm. "And that's the reason why."

"Judy, has he gotten any sleep the last few days?"

I was flushed with embarrassment. "I don't know. We sometimes sleep in separate rooms."

"I've not had any sleep, but that's not the point." Then Joe's face became tender as he looked at me. "I don't know what's going to happen to us. But you need to know the truth. Mary is my wife. She's been fine with us living together. I just don't know your place in this whole thing."

Brian said, "Is that why you're not wearing your wedding ring, Joe?"

"Yes. It was bothering me, and I didn't need it. I don't want to hurt Judy. But it's all clear to me now."

"Hey, Joe. You and I have been friends for a long time, haven't we?" Brian said. Joe nodded his head. "Would you trust me to help?"

"It depends. I'll have to think about it."

"Look, I'm not a doctor, but I know it's time to get help. I've never seen you like this."

"I'm fine. I don't need help."

"Well, how about you and I just take a ride." He tried to coax him. We feared he'd get in his vehicle.

"No, I'm fine. I can handle this on my own. I need to go to the mountains. That's what I did last time. When we're finished here, that's where I'm heading."

"Judy told me she bailed you out of jail for speeding on the highway."

"Yeah, she did. I had to speed. They were chasing me."

"So how can we keep that from happening again?" The more questions we asked, the more agitated he got.

Joe didn't fit criteria for mandatory admission. The church provided him a hotel room for the night. He'd be safe and able to get sleep there. He agreed to give Brian his car keys if he promised not to give them to me.

I used my extra set to drive the vehicle and secretly park it in a friend's driveway. It would be deadly if he drove 110 miles an hour on the highway again. Food was still on the table when I walked into the empty house. I changed the passwords of our debit and credit cards.

I silently asked myself, *What am I doing here? My life is a lie. I don't belong.* I felt the same eerie detachment I'd felt as a young mom, before my confession to Richard.

Two days later, Joe qualified for mandatory inpatient treatment.[86] That was the morning Dr. Morgan called. I had a full day of clients and a presentation that evening with twenty attendees. I was thankful this wasn't a first time to speak. My PowerPoint was ready.

When I got home, I listened to Joe's phone message. His loving voice made me hopeful. The clarity and smoothness of the presentation comforted me. God showed me His care. I must have been floating on the prayers of friends and family. But the house was dark like that cottage in Canada. I couldn't dance. Instead, I looked for my blue leather Bible and picked up the brown hardback journal with acid-free gilded pages.

---

86 As mentioned in chapter 1, mandatory treatment is involuntary admittance to a hospital when a person is out of touch with reality and may be in danger to themselves or others.

Chapter 24

DANCE OF MENTAL ILLNESS

*And those who were seen dancing were thought
to be insane by those who could not hear the music.*
—Friedrich Nietzsche

Anosognosia is a condition in the brain's prefrontal cortex that prevents insights and accurate self-perceptions. It affects 40 percent of those with bipolar disorder and 50 percent of those with schizophrenia. What we judge as resistance or stubbornness may instead be a physiological impossibility.[87] When a spouse has poor insight over their personal narratives, the messiness in marriage is even more challenging. Along with "normal" statistics

---

87 Xavier Amador, PhD, *I Am Not Sick I Don't Need Help! How to Help Someone with Mental Illness Accept Treatment* (New York: Vida Press, 2011). I listened to Dr. Amador's book twice in the midst of Joe's second episode. This resource is now a staple in my office. Learning about anosognosia has zoned me into reality about the illness, symptoms, and aftermath of psychosis.

that indicate risk for marriage, spouses with bipolar disorder are 90 percent more likely to divorce.[88]

Those who live with the delicacy and fierceness of mental illness need fortress strength in their partnerships with each other. It's absolutely essential to have community support and compliance to treatment. Otherwise, the non-ill spouse's health is at stake.

Of course, full disclosure from a potential partner is crucial. But for those with severe mental illness, even more so. The insights of those closest to them can give clarity about their learned dances. People of a partner's past and present relationships may give valuable perspectives considering the presence of anosognosia both during and beyond episodes.

Even though many people experience estrangement from their family of origins or former friends, it's important for all of us to be in, and grow through, significant relationships. Friends, coworkers, relatives, and other people are mirrors to our souls. Without them, we cannot grow our character or gain wisdom. It usually takes therapy and support groups to get us out of isolation. Moving beyond messy relationships is worth the journey to our authentic selves.

"Those who live with the delicacy and fierceness of mental illness need fortress strength in their partnerships with each other. It's absolutely essential to have community support and compliance to treatment. Otherwise, the non-ill spouse's health is at stake."

We all have limited self-awareness because we experience the world and others through our filters. None of us has a corner on all truth. Even as I wrote this book, my editor and coach warned me that someone

---

88   I want to focus on the 10 percent who are likely to have a growing marriage and be instrumental in changing those discouraging statistics. This is a Psych Central article written by Therese J. Borchard, https://psychcentral.com/blog/being-married-to-a-person-with-depression-or-bipolar-6-survival-tips/.

close is likely to say, "That's not how it happened." Of which I'm to respond, "You're right. That's not how it happened to you. That's how it happened to me."[89] And those who challenge another's experiences can choose to write their own stories. It's important to honor our differences and respect unique experiences and viewpoints of others.

Just as in the story of six blind men describing an elephant, we must consider partial truths and honor another's viewpoint.

One blind man feels the side of the elephant and describes it like a wall. The other who feels the tail says, "No, you're wrong. It's like a rope."

The other who felt the tusk said, "You're both wrong. It's like a sword."

The fourth blind man who felt the ear said, "No. It's like a fan."

After feeling the leg, the fifth man said, "You're all wrong. It's like a tree."

The sixth one felt the trunk. "No, it's like a snake."

All the blind men were right in their experiences of the elephant. And we need to consider the unique perspectives of others as we relate in that space between our differences.

"Even though many people experience estrangement from their family of origins or former friends, it's important for all of us to be in, and grow through, significant relationships."

---

89   Marion Roach Smith's website is https://marionroach.com.

I spoke through the opening in the glass partition. "I'm here to see my husband. He's #1469." All visitors needed the patient code to protect privacy. A young technician handed me a clipboard.

"Sign here. You can't bring anything in with you. You'll need to lock up your belongings." She pointed to the opposite wall with lockers big enough for a coat or purse.

"I brought him a change of clothes." I gave her the plastic bag.

She opened it and looked through all the pockets. "I'll make sure he gets it."

"Thanks." I signed my name in the visitor column and #1469 in the patient column. Then I opened the locker door and traded my purse for the plastic spiral wristband with a key attached. It locked automatically when I shut it. Awkward moments later, a jingle of keys and footsteps signaled my membership into a new group. A worker unlocked the steel door. Some of the visitors took a left down the hall to the first and second levels of care. But my group took a right toward the acute care unit. Another jingle of keys unlocked another steel door. My Joe was in the hallway looking for me. We smiled, and I felt relief.

With a quick embrace he took my hand and peeked in the common room. "It's too crowded in there." He took charge like he did at Swing Fest as if looking for an open space on a crowded dance floor. But this crowd was a room full of disheveled patients and tense visitors. I didn't like this dance party.

Joe asked a nurse, "Can we visit across the hall in my room? We need privacy."

"Well, you're not supposed to." The nurse gave us a wink. "But I won't tell if you do. Keep the door open."

His room was adjacent to the common room with a wide doorway a few feet away. "Keep the lights off. They irritate my eyes." The fluorescent lights from the hallway were enough to lighten the dark room. He acted like a freshman college student proud to show off his dorm room. "What do you think? I had it all to myself last night."

"Great. Did you get any sleep?"

"No, I've not slept in three days. I can't sleep here."

"Do you want me to bring your pillow and blanket?"

He was annoyed at my questions. "No, I won't be here long. I need my socks. Did you bring a pair?"

"Yes. I left them at the front desk. And I packed your toothbrush and other clothes. They'll bring them to you."

"I won't need all that. I'll be outta here by tomorrow." We sat on the side of his single bed facing the doorway. "They don't know what they're doing around here. I've never been able to sleep in a hospital. Judy, you need to talk to the doctor and get me outta here. I won't get better here. I need my own bed and I'll be fine."

"The main thing is that you get the help you need."

"Shh…don't say anything. Just listen to me. I need to tell you about private things. This is stuff I've known for a long time. That's why we didn't need to go in there." He pointed toward the door. "Just listen. Promise you'll trust me."

"Okay."

"Shh…now stop interrupting. You've got to let me talk. You always interrupt and don't listen. You've got to be still." I became aware of my slightest gestures. I nodded and gave him the same compassion I did for my clients who needed to be heard and understood. I could do this for Joe. His speech was pressured. "You need to listen and follow my lead."

"Okay." I was proud of myself for being calm. He verbalized thoughts that sounded like a scene from the *Starship Enterprise*. Joe has always enjoyed sci-fi movies like *Star Trek*.[90] He was fascinated with the latest research and space science discoveries.

---

90   Just in case you're interested, here's more: https://en.wikipedia.org/wiki/Star_Trek_(film_series).

When he paused for my response, I said, "Joe, you need to trust the doctors. They can help. The medicine will be good for—"

"You always interrupt me!" he said in a louder voice. "Now listen. You've never had an experience like this. I can't expect you to understand. This is mystical. It's a mystery to me. You'll need to trust me. Do you?"

How could I balance my truth with his? "Joe, I trust the real you. We need to get you well."

"Stop interrupting!" He startled me, and I was getting scared. I nodded again, trying to keep my face relaxed while I faced the open door.

He softened. "I don't know what this means for the two of us. I love you and I always will. Don't you remember me telling you about my first girlfriend when I was five?"

I nodded and took a deep breath.

"Remember I told you her name was Mary?" He paused to get another head nod. "We were Joseph and Mary back then." He smiled as if I got it. My head betrayed me. I did remember his girlfriend, Mary. And I'd had "divine moments" myself. Joe and I talked about them before.

"It's all making sense now. This has been my purpose all along. It's mystical but it's true." He talked faster. "The medicine they're trying to give me is poison. I've got to keep my mind clear. I have special powers that no one else has. And I can't let them mess with it." Then he stood with a dreamy look on his face. He hugged himself and his eyes moistened. "Mary is my wife. I've had a soul bond with her ever since I was nineteen. I can't explain it to you. This isn't possible with you or anyone." He swayed as if he were holding his lover. When he saw my face, his mood switched.

"You look pensive."

"Well, I've never seen you like this before."

"That's because I've never felt like this with anyone. I've never given my heart to you. It's always been with Mary. My purpose is to be a priest. Don't you remember me telling you I almost became a monk?"

"Well, yeah. That was a long time ago."

"As soon as I get out of here, we'll get an annulment. And I don't know if you'll have a part in this plan with the universe. You'll need to get me out of here first. Some of the patients here know exactly what I mean. But the doctors don't."

"I hear you." My body was tense.

With a blank stare, he said. "You don't trust me, do you?"

"Joe, I trust you when you're well."

"You're one of them, aren't you?"

"No, I'm not. You can trust me." Gosh, what was I saying? I looked through the wide doorway and stood up. "I love you, Joe. It's time for me to go. We'll talk tomorrow. Remember, I brought you a change of clothes. I hope you appreciate that." I walked into the fluorescent lights in the hall. He followed beside me.

"I do. Thank you. You need to go. You make me nervous."

We hugged each other. But I clung a little longer through our goodbyes. Maybe the warmth of my body close to his would penetrate the delusions. "Go on. I need some rest."

I waited with my new group members. That jingle of keys cued my anticipation of an unlocked steel door. I looked back at him with our half-smiles meeting along with my pensive face. Then I turned and walked through the door a few paces behind the others. The hallway tile floor echoed the click... click... click... click... click of my shoes. Under my breath, I chanted with its rhythm. Truth... truth... truth... truth... truth.

The worker unlocked the door to the lobby. I unlocked the small locker, took out my purse, and left the spiral wristband key inside. Then I walked through the unlocked door to reality outside.

Chapter 25

DANCE OF DELUSIONS

*...There are only two things strong enough to keep you
inside the dance of life: Great love and great suffering.*
—Father Richard Rohr

O f all the emotions we identify as temporary guests, sadness is the most lingering. Psychologist and researcher Joseph Forgas tells us that mild sadness improves memory, judgment, and motivation.[91] It can help us be more compassionate and reach out to those in need. The longevity of most emotions is ninety seconds. But sadness can last up to five days before turning into despair or depression. The character, Sadness, was the little blue girl in the movie *Inside Out.*

---

91 Joseph Forgas, "Four Ways Sadness May Be Good for You," 2014, https://
greatergood.berkeley.edu/article/item/four_ways_sadness_may_be_good_for_you.

She motivated Riley, the main character, to return home from her runaway attempt.[92]

"As we face the darkness of our humanity, we need to be even more intentional to hear the messages of our temporary emotions."

Again, we must allow all emotions to cycle through our hearts. Our task is to keep them from becoming permanent guests. As we face the darkness of our humanity, we need to be even more intentional to hear the messages of our temporary emotions. Efforts to maintain constant happiness actually keep us stuck. When we numb out unpleasant reactions, we're unaware of divine invitations. Instead, we need to allow the wisdom those difficult feelings provide. And it's true that God never wastes any of our pain. Without it, we miss our authentic selves.

———————

The brown hardback journal sat on the table as I turned to familiar Scripture passages in my blue leather Bible. More teardrops mixed the ink of my thoughts. What had Joe held in his subconscious mind all his life? What were his private thoughts in his contemplative prayers each morning?

How could I tell my sons and daughters of Joe's condition? The grandchildren wouldn't be allowed to come over and spend the night. My long-distance daughter was the first to know. All four became concerned for my well-being. I tried so hard to let them live their own

---

92 *Inside Out* Movie is not only my granddaughter's favorite, but it also provides accurate neuroscience to help both kids and adults respect all emotions. Plus, it confirms my analogy of necessary and temporary guests in our human psyches. See https://www.gse.harvard.edu/news/uk/15/09/brain-science-inside-out.

adult lives. I didn't want them to get sucked into the black hole of their parent's troubled relationship. Now I was the needy parent for them to feel sorry for. All this made me mad.

I rearranged my schedule for the next day's visiting hours. The worker opened the envelope with photos I brought to give Joe. We visited in the common room, and I read his birthday card aloud. We smiled together at pictures of us dancing, canoeing, and camping. On the next day's visit, I asked, "Where's your birthday card? And where are the pictures?"

"Oh, I threw them away."

"What?"

"I didn't need them anymore. I can't have extra things like that lying around."

"Really?"

"It's okay. I appreciated you giving them to me. But I don't need clutter. And it makes me nervous."

"Oh…I'm wondering. What did you do with your wedding ring?"

"I threw it away!"

"You what?"

"Yeah, I didn't need that either. All that stuff lying around messes with my mind."

"Where is it now? The ring?"

"I don't know. It's probably on the floorboard. It doesn't matter."

"It DOES matter!" I couldn't be nice anymore.

Joe's best friend Steve joined the visitor club to see him. I was more than ready for him to take my place. It had been over a week, and I'd had enough. I went out of my way to get him everything he asked, hoping my empathy, hugs, and gifts would make a difference. But it didn't matter. He refused medication, and I wasn't playing his games anymore.

I walked out the door into reality and waited in the car under a shade tree. A half hour later, Steve came out with his head down and his shoulders slumped. He looked up, and I motioned for him to sit in the passenger seat. "How was your visit?"

"Wow, Judy," he said, shaking his head. "I had no idea it was this bad." He teared up. "I'm so sorry. This isn't the Joe we know. I can't imagine what you're going through. But I've lost my best friend. I just don't know what to say."

I was stoic. "I'm thankful you've been a good friend to Joe." Steve's sorrow softened me. We both cried, and I handed him a tissue. But this felt like condolences at a funeral. I was the widow who had already grieved but comforted others.

I found the dirty wedding ring on the floorboard. And I discovered more lies in the prelude to his episode. One of his friends told me that Joe bragged about not sleeping in forty-eight hours. But I remembered asking him directly before the conference. He told me the opposite. He texted his agnostic/atheist friend and asked *him* for prayer. But he didn't trust me, his Christian wife, to pray for him. In my journal, I wrote a letter he'd never read.

> *I paid a high price trusting you as my husband. I'll pick up the pieces of my life and be one of those twice-divorced Imago therapists. I'll have major heartache, and I'll continue to meet God in those jagged pieces of my soul. Like Andrew's clay cup that fell off the counter. Perhaps God can make a beautiful mosaic out of it. I don't know if I could ever dance again if you choose not to be my partner.*

Joe's calls became harsher and more demanding when I didn't respond immediately. My phone was off when I spent time with the grandchildren. I became "one of them." He accused me of being a pest to the nurses when I called to check on him. Then he signed documents for his legal rights to cut me off from communications with his doctors.

I faced the possibility that he may never comply with treatment. Even if he did, I feared too much brain damage would have happened by now. He'd never be the Joe I married. He insisted that we get an annulment so he could become a Catholic priest. And I consulted with divorce attorneys.

At the end of a counseling day, a social worker called. "Your husband asked me to call you to set up a family meeting. Can you come tomorrow at 2:30?"

I looked at whom I could reschedule. "Yes, I'll be there," I said. Maybe I'd know whether or not Joe complied to treatment.

Many of my client files had the note "rescheduled due to counselor family emergency." Some were in Joe's group. They looked to him as a role model since he was their facilitator. *What do I tell these clients?*

"I heard that your husband's in the hospital. Is he okay?"

"I don't know. This has been tough." I couldn't tell them that he refused me privileged communications. If he ever led this group again, I wouldn't recommend it to my clients.

One new client was like a female version of Joe. I tried thinking of her as a "divine appointment." What counselor would have more insight into her marriage and how difficult it was for her spouse? But after a few sessions, her intensity wore me out.

I loved doing therapy group work more than individual counseling. But my previous joy of facilitating the "Mindful Mood" group also drained me. How could I show up *authentic*? How much more could I empathize with their struggles and give them hope?

I became aware of other cases that drained me. Some of my client sessions helped me get out of my own despair. They showed me God's transformation and human resilience. I remembered Dr. Benner's statement: "God's love is not enough. It must be received." My therapist and friends told me, "You can't do for others what only they can do for themselves."

The next day, I signed my name to the visitor column and #1469 in the patient column. I brought in note-taking supplies, a writing pad, and pen. The conference room was straight ahead with no right turn down the tile hallway. The large windows facing the hall had a glass door in between. It welcomed transparency unlike the locked steel doors hiding a different reality.

Eye contact was brief when Joe and I saw each other. What a contrast to my initial relief with our first meeting in the acute unit.

"Mrs. Herman, I'm Amy, your husband's social worker." We met with a kind and firm handshake along with direct eye contact.

"I'm glad to put a voice with the person." Determined to stay in my reality, I couldn't pretend with normal pleasantries.

"This is Alecia, our executive director." We recognized each other from grad school.

"I remember you."

"Yes, I remember you too, Judy."

Our faithful priest, Brian, walked in with repeat introductions. We sat down, and Amy began. "Your husband wants to be discharged today, and we need your feedback."

"Okay. But I don't know the purpose of this meeting," I said, ready to take notes. Having facilitated groups for years, I was aware of every nuance. All participants have a right to know why they're meeting. "I've had no privileged communications about his treatment. Last I knew, he's not been compliant."

Joe took charge in his usual way. "They can't hold me here. I'm going to the dance tomorrow night. I'm playing the music like I do every month. I'd like you to be there with me."

"You're not serious. This isn't happening." I looked at Alecia, Amy, and Brian for some kind of affirmation. To Joe, I said, "I already emailed the board, and they don't expect you there."

"Joe began his medications two days ago," Amy reported.

Alecia said, "Judy, even though he's not as well as we'd like him to be, he has a choice to leave. He doesn't qualify for mandatory treatment since he met with the judge this morning."

Nothing I said mattered, and I wouldn't allow him to come home. They discharged him and convinced me that his staying in our pop-up camper was a good option. He promised to tell our friends where he'd be but refused to tell me. He wanted an annulment and expected me to dance with him as usual.

Joe and our friend Marcia shared camaraderie serving on the board of our local USA dance chapter.[93] His job was to choose the music playlist with just the right tempo and variety for our monthly dances. But he missed the planning meeting.

I composed a discreet email to the group so they could get a substitute for Friday's dance. But Joe insisted on being there as he had every month for the last three years. He expected me to meet him there and be our jovial selves. I didn't feel like dancing, but I needed to warn our friends.

While in the foxtrot line, I said to Marcia, "Joe's just been released from the psychiatric hospital yesterday."

"Oh, Judy. I'm so sorry."

"Yeah, I wanted to protect his privacy. Did you get the group email?"

"Yes, I read it. John was ready to take his place tonight."

"Yeah, I know. Marcia, this has been the darkest days of my life." I tried keeping conversation light since we were there to have fun.

"Oh, I can imagine. I couldn't trust my ex, who was bipolar." I didn't want Marcia to think Joe was like her ex-husband.

"His brother keeps telling me that it's the illness. It's not Joe. But I'm struggling. Does he seem uptight to you?" We looked his way.

"Yeah, he does. A little more than usual."

---

93 http://www.usadance.org

As we inched our way up the waltz line, she took Pierre's hand to dance around the floor. I took Jeff's and pretended that Joe was okay.

This "sickness" fooled me. Joe chose to take his medications. He played music for the dance and laughed like his normal self. After the dance I drove home to a dark, empty house.

I filled my journal we carefully chose together. I didn't remember its original purpose.

> *Dear Joe,*
>
> *I told you I had peace about this decision for an annulment. But I need for you to understand that my heart is being ripped out of my chest over the last twenty-one days. I will not be able to come home to this house after living the happiest days of my life with you here. I'm unable to maintain this home as a place for grandchildren to visit. Our union as husband and wife and any involvement in each other's lives will end when the divorce is final. I'll have to pick up the pieces of my life since I'm experiencing you with such disregard for our union. The Joe I was married to was bonded with me soul to soul. Neither of us could bear the thought of living without the other.*
>
> *I'm experiencing this "alien" who has occupied Joe's body. This other person is heartless, irresponsible, hedonistic, and selfish. I've never known my husband in that way. I'm saying "goodbye" to the warm, kind-hearted, loving Joe I've always known. I'm divorcing the "alien" and will have nothing to do with the one who took away the soul of my beloved, Joe.*
>
> *Prayerfully,*
> *Judy*

My conscience wouldn't allow me to divorce Joe before he was well. Instead, I wrote it all in black and white with handwritten words.

Chapter 26

DANCE OF THE "D" WORD

'Tis better to have loved and lost than never to have loved at all.
—Alfred Lord Tennyson

T he Gottman Institute provides us with a diagram of a Sound Relationship House.[94] The walls that hold everything else in place are trust and commitment. If one wall is missing, efforts to get beyond the messiness are futile.

Couples who come in for counseling seek help in one of three major categories: crisis mode, control mode, or construction mode. The first is crisis mode. Therapy is their last resort. If it doesn't work, one or the other has made plans for a catastrophic exit like divorce.

Crisis mode is not the same as counseling. Most couples on the verge of divorce need additional help to get them out of crisis mode. A marital

---

94   For more about the Sound Relationship House, https://www.gottman.com/about/the-gottman-method/.

crisis is not the same as a mental health crisis. Even programs such as Retrouvaille or Getting the Love You Want require both spouses to be self-aware and intentional. The weekend intensives are not appropriate for those who have secret affairs, severe addictions, depression, or mania. Rather, it's crucial to get out of crisis mode and assess the damage before counseling can begin.

Some therapists are more skilled than others in handling crisis cases. But do not assume that crisis management is the same as counseling.

Unfortunately, some claim that couples counseling leads to divorce. But they don't take into account that going to counseling, for some, is a last resort.[95] Also, many counselors do not have insight or additional training about emotional and verbal abuse issues. That's why I encourage couples to take Gottman's assessment,[96] which helps a therapist sort out mental health as well as relationship issues affecting the couple. As mentioned in chapter 10, couples counseling is not appropriate if certain other issues interfere. Rather, it causes more damage to both individuals if underlying manipulation, secrecy, fear, or a mental health crisis is going on.

Three Major Categories for Couples Seeking Help

- Crisis Mode
- Control Mode
- Construction Mode

---

95 "4 Reasons Marriage Counseling Leads to Divorce," https://www. theadventurouswriter.com/quipstipsrelationships/reasons-why-marriage-counseling-leads-to-divorce/.

96 The Gottman Relationship Checkup takes about two hours to answer a series of questions. The trained Gottman therapist will meet with each individually after the couple's initial session: https://checkup.gottman.com.

The second major category is the control mode. One feels the need for change and the other doesn't. Neither wants to divorce, but if they don't get help, one is sure the marriage is heading in that direction. An undercurrent agenda of "social engineering" prevails. One wants the comfort of sameness while the other wants necessary change. They may be stuck in the control/submission dance.

The last major category is the construction mode. Premarital or newlywed couples come in to make sure they're on the right track. Or the couple is transitioning into another phase like parenthood, empty-nest, or blended families. They both want to build healthy and growing partnership habits. Some come in to establish the counselor/client relationship as a patient would for her primary care physician. When issues arise, they have familiarity and trust of the counselor and therapy process.

None of us wants to talk about the "D" word. Whether that "D" means death or divorce, it's a subject we avoid. But if we don't face endings, we're unable to become unstuck from our relationship messes.

Henry Cloud addresses necessary endings in business and other significant relationships.[97] Again, it's important to honor the worth, value, and dignity of both individuals in a relationship. To get beyond the messiness, necessary endings might indicate an old marriage is not working. It needs to change. The change may be a divorce from toxic patterns, reactions, and unhealthy dances. We need to say goodbye to the old

> "Necessary endings might indicate an old marriage is not working... The change may be a divorce from toxic patterns, reactions, and unhealthy dances."

---

97   Henry Cloud, *Necessary Endings: The Employees, Businesses, and Relationships That All of Us Have to Give Up in Order to Move Forward* (New York: HarperBusiness, 2011).

and hello to different ways of being. Otherwise, the commitment to a destructive marriage degrades both individuals. And it keeps them blinded from divine invitations to their authentic selves. The long-term toxicity in the relationship also accounts for stress-related illness or even premature death.

———————

I hoped Joe would get better on his own at his secret campsite. Steve visited with him around the campfire, and I asked him to call me when he left.

"How is he? Is he getting better?"

A long silence followed. "I'm sorry, Judy. I need to keep my promise. I don't want to tell you too much."

"Please, Steve. I've already talked to attorneys. I've got to know how to prepare."

He opened up. "I had to be careful not to become 'one of them.' So I just let him talk."

"Can you tell if he's still on medication?"

"I didn't ask, but I would guess not. There's still a lot of delusions." When I heard that, I was so angry. He went on medications to be well enough for the dance. He DID have choices.

"What did he say about me? Does he still want an annulment? Or a divorce? What are his feelings about me? I hate to put you on the spot."

He hesitated. "I don't want to hurt your feelings, Judy. I know this is hard for you."

"Please don't worry about hurting my feelings. At this point, there's nothing you could say that would hurt more."

"Well… he said it was no love lost. But you know these are delusions."

"Yeah, yeah, I know. Thanks for telling me, Steve. You're likely the only friend he trusts."

"I need to tell you something else. He put a down payment on a motorcycle. He plans to pick it up as soon as his new credit card arrives. Said he's buying it from his dealer friend he's known for years. And we know it's likely to take his life."

I had to stop him. The next day I took a copy of Joe's discharge papers and approached the dealer.

He looked at me. "Ma'am, you're not the only wife who thinks her husband is crazy for buying a motorcycle."

"Don't you see this?" I pointed to the papers.

"I'm sorry, ma'am. Like I said, you're not the only wife who's come in here trying to stop her husband from buying a bike. He's already put money down. He signed a contract."

I couldn't convince the man that I had nothing against motorcycles. He obviously didn't care whether someone died on a bike he sold them the day before. How hardhearted could this businessperson be? I was trying to save my husband's life. I was so mad when I left that store. My desperation and persuasion dances were useless.

That night I wrote a letter to Joe in the journal meant for love letters.

Your "friend" selling you the motorcycle is just as mentally ill as you. I tried keeping you from your delusional self. I don't have the stamina anymore. I'm weary of grieving. I have no more heaving sobs and groans. The deep places of my heart are too broken. I need to move on. Have fun buying your motorcycle, Joe Herman. Maybe your soul is still there. I don't know.

Worst-case scenario, if he got in an accident and died, I would grieve. But if he caused another's death, how could I live with myself? My only choice was to prepare for widowhood or life as a second-time divorcee. But a small part of me believed my Joe would come back.

One morning my phone woke me up at five o'clock with a number I didn't recognize.

"Hello?"

"Is this Mrs. Herman?"

"Yes, who's calling?"

"I'm the emergency room nurse. Your husband's been in an accident."

"Oh my gosh. Is he alive?"

"Yes, yes. I'll be leaving my shift, and he asked me to call."

"What happened?"

"He arrived about midnight. EMTs are amazed he's alive. He has minor injuries and will be sore the next few days."

"What? Why didn't you call before?"

"He didn't want us to. But he's just been discharged and is ready for you to pick him up."

"What happened?"

"His car ran into a concrete guardrail. He was covered in gasoline, and they had to use the Jaws of Life to pull him out."

"Were others involved?"

"No, it was a single-car accident."

"I'll be right there." I hung up the phone and dressed quickly. With a sigh of relief, I called 911 for a police escort, and I called Steve. "He *will* go directly from the ER back to the psychiatric hospital," I told him.

Details of his accident were sketchy since the nurses and doctors had left their shift. The vehicle turned over twice and landed upside down. Like a crushed tin can it had a small bulge on the driver's side. There were no reports of Joe driving under the influence.

I thanked the officer, and Joe agreed to ride with Steve to the psychiatric hospital. The four-hour admission process and near-death accident weren't enough evidence for mandatory admission. Joe was masterful at the persuasion dance. I called Brian. It took his testimony to convince clinicians of Joe's danger to himself and others.

In another journal letter I wrote:

I'm tired of feeling this sick feeling in the pit of my stomach. I'm tired of waking up in the morning with the realization that the nightmare is REAL. I'm tired of reliving the same excruciating pain from my first damn marriage. I wish I could feel sorry for you, but I'm too angry, too angry, too angry. STOP playing games! STOP IT. I've never had a client as bad off as you.

I didn't believe Ralph, Joe's brother, anymore. "It's the sickness, Judy. It's not him. He's a more compassionate human being than I ever was."

I gave up on writing letters to Joe. Instead, I wrote lists of "reasons for divorce." I put an "I" to indicate "illness" next to deal breakers like "deception." And I put a "C" next to character traits like "extremely persuasive." Some had both "I" and "C" as I tried to make sense of my insane marriage.

Our union was a small blip on my timeline. Three decades and four children didn't compare. I had no significant history with Joe. That first marriage was a different darkness. But both were too dark for me. My prayers came out.

I didn't sign up for this. This is not what I said "I do" to. Does this even fall into the category of betrayal? Has our marriage been fraudulent all this time? Could I possibly live with myself for divorcing a man who doesn't have all his rational thinking in place?

Now that he was back in the hospital, I'd wait until he was well before retaining an attorney. I called Ralph so he could take over Joe's responsibilities for their mother, who was in assisted living. I would no longer be her power of attorney. We cried together on the phone. "He's my brother, Judy. I can't divorce my brother. But I understand if you need to. I'm just so sorry." I called our realtor for the resale value of our home. I'd find a place closer to the grandchildren.

The social worker called requesting another meeting, even though I still had no privileged communications. Steve agreed to be there. The hospital system and I didn't trust each other.

The man who took over Joe's body cleaned up and looked less like a psychiatric patient. He was eager to see me like a used-car salesman about to close a deal. Another man said, "Hello, Mrs. Herman. I'm Jeff, your husband's social worker."

"Where's Amy? I thought *she* was his social worker."

"She's no longer on his case. They assigned it to me yesterday." This guy looked fresh out of college, but I shook his hand firmly.

"Great," I said sarcastically. "I'm sure this was a difficult case for her."

"Judy bothered the whole staff. She kept calling and wearing everybody out," Joe said.

"That was before Joe refused for me to know about his treatment. I haven't called since." We sounded like two little kids tattling on each other. "Are we waiting for Alecia?"

"I'm sorry, but she's in another meeting. We don't have long, so let's get started." Jeff tried taking control.

"So why are we meeting?" I knew the obvious. But they needed to be clear.

"The doctor agreed to discharge me," Joe said.

I looked at Jeff. "My husband is NOT well. He is NOT ready to come home. You DO know he almost died in a car accident because he was discharged. Do you have that in your notes?"

"That was an accident," Joe said. "It had nothing to do with being sick. I thought the guardrail was a lane."

Jeff flipped through his file folder. "I don't see that in his records. So we can't take it into account."

"Are you kidding me? Joe is NOT safe! He WILL get in another accident."

Steve spoke up. "He's planning to buy a motorcycle. Sorry, Joe. But that's a concern for your safety."

"I promise you, I can't ride it anyway," Joe said, trying to convince Steve and me. "I'm too sore from the accident." To Jeff, he said, "I've never hurt anyone. And I've never been suicidal. I'm perfectly fine. And I need to sleep in my own bed."

Jeff said, "We need to make some kind of agreement. And we need to do it in the next few minutes. What are you willing to do?"

Joe looked at me. "Can you stay with your mom and dad? I promise, I'll be better in a few days once I get the rest I need."

"I'm not comfortable with you coming home until you're stable."

"I'm sorry, Mrs. Herman, but your husband doesn't qualify for mandatory treatment," Jeff said. The motorcycle issue didn't faze him. "We won't be able to address all this today. The decision to discharge your husband has already been made. If he can't come home, we need to find arrangements for him. You can settle on the other issues later."

"I can stay in the camper like I did before," Joe said.

"No, you can't," I countered. "It's not there anymore. Brian and I brought it back home."

I turned to Jeff. "So my only choice is to let Joe come home."

Then to Joe, "You need to promise me you won't drink alcohol. I don't even know what meds you're on. And you know alcohol would interfere."

Negotiations went back and forth. Joe promised the social worker and Steve that he wouldn't drink alcohol. He would continue his medications. His vehicle was totaled so he couldn't drive anyway. He would stay at the house and sleep in his own bed. I agreed to stay with my parents until I felt comfortable to go home. Steve agreed to check in with him the next few days.

I had no other choice than to comply with the system. That evening Steve texted me after helping Joe get settled at the house. I called him right back.

"How is he? Did he drink?"

"I'm sorry. But he did drink a bottle of wine."

"What? He promised! That was the condition for him to come home. He lied to you and the social worker and me! How could he? Didn't you hear him say he kept his promises?"

"I…I didn't know what to do. I'm so sorry."

How could Steve let him do that? I imagined my raised voice intimidated him. But I was so mad.

My influence didn't matter. Joe was soon to be my ex-husband. I planned a divorce on the day of our five-year anniversary. This was clearer than my twenty-eight-year anniversary date when I went to Canada. I had no other choice.

Chapter 27

DANCE OF GRIEF

*The body is a sacred garment. It's your first and last garment; it
is what you enter life in and what you depart life with, and it
should be treated with honor.*

—Martha Graham

Psychosis is a condition in the mind in which a person loses contact with reality. Delusions (false beliefs) and/or hallucinations (sensing things that others don't) are symptoms of psychosis, which is not a stand-alone diagnosis. Beyond the severe form of bipolar disorder and schizophrenia, psychosis can occur from other factors. They include:

Sleep deprivation
Adverse reaction to medications
Head injury

Epilepsy
Thyroid disorders
Substance abuse
Deficiency in vitamin B-12
Postpartum depression

Mark Lukach, author of *My Lovely Wife in the Psych Ward*,[98] gives comfort and hope through his memoir about his wife's psychosis. Dr. Xavier Amador[99] shares how he connected with his brother who had schizophrenia. He grieved the brother's former self and accepted his illness. It required a new relationship between them. Both books increased my compassion and wisdom while struggling through our crisis.

And Elisabeth Kübler-Ross[100] has taught us the stages of grief. We need to cycle through the shock, denial, anger, depression, and acceptance. There will be a before and after. And whether it happens suddenly or over time, our acceptance is crucial. Things are not supposed to go back to how they used to be.

———————

"I promised these guys I'd buy it. They've held it for a week. I can't break my promise." Joe's pleas about the motorcycle continued.

———————

98 Both Joe and I read this book while recovering after his second episode. It gave us a point of reference. For me, I regained hope, compassion, and courage when I couldn't see beyond the despair: http://www.marklukach.com.

99 Dr. Amador's website can be found at http://dramador.com/about-dr-amador/. This TedX talk will arouse emotions and empathy for understanding of what we would otherwise judge as resistance: https://www.youtube.com/watch?v=NXxytf6kfPM.

100 Now deceased, Dr. Kübler-Ross has long been a staple for graduate degree programs and therapist trainings on grief. This link takes you to the Elisabeth Kübler-Ross Foundation: https://www.ekrfoundation.org/elisabeth-kubler-ross/.

"Oh, so it's okay to break your promise to me, the social worker, and your best friend? You promised *them* you wouldn't drink alcohol. How does that make sense?"

"That's different."

"You can count on a divorce if you do." I was serious. Joe bought it anyway and "promised" not to ride until he was well.

The next day we sat with Joe's therapist. I asked, "Where's the line between sickness and free will? And I need to know because I'm about to retain an attorney. Joe bought a motorcycle knowing I would divorce him if he did."

"I promised you I wouldn't ride it. I'm too sore from the accident anyway."

"That means nothing." We sounded like the two kids tattling again.

Dr. Burns gently interrupted. His slow speech de-escalated our tension. "I strongly advise that both of you don't make major decisions now. And here's why. Outrageous beliefs are easier to get over." He looked at me. "We know that Joe is no longer experiencing these. But irrational ideas within the realm of possibility will be more difficult for him to sort out." He turned to Joe. "Your buying this motorcycle is one of those irrational ideas."

"I couldn't go back on my word to my dealer friend. And I promised Judy I wouldn't ride it. I don't even know how to ride a motorcycle."

Dr. Burns was able to rationalize with Joe. "Didn't you promise Judy that you wouldn't drink alcohol?"

"Yes. I did. I had to so I could stay at home while she stayed with her parents."

"You know that's lying."

"That's different."

"Joe, you need to know that your promises don't mean anything now. Judy can't trust that you'll tell the truth."

Joe paused like an elementary child trying to figure out a math problem. "Oh. I think I get it."

Then Dr. Burns spoke to me. "See what I mean? This isn't easy for you, Judy. But I don't think his buying a motorcycle has anything to do with your marriage."

"How could it not? Joe still wants to be a Catholic priest and get an annulment."

"Yes, and that's another irrational idea. There's no way of knowing how long this will take. It could be weeks or years. And sometimes never. Expect Joe to be fatigued and have mental sluggishness for a few months."

A couple months later he sold the motorcycle he never rode. I researched the effects of psychosis on the brain. I developed more compassion for my clients, and Joe began to grieve. He wanted to be my husband. He cleaned up and wore his wedding ring. I wasn't convinced that divorce was the answer. The indecision tormented us both.

"Had I known I'd put you through all this, I would never have married you. I'm so sorry, Judy." That was the most honest statement I had heard from him since before the episode. I couldn't expect him to work on the marriage. But I could lean into reality with him.

During Easter Sunday's service, I was overcome with the resurrection message. I made an intentional choice to believe it was a divine invitation. God could resurrect our marriage. And I couldn't do it for us both. It would take two.

We danced monthly while Joe programmed music as before. We camped in our pop-up, rode our bikes, and took hikes and canoe trips.

I educated my family about bipolar disorder. Joe's psychosis was as valid a sickness as any other physical sickness. We both met with an attorney, who documented our wills. Joe appointed me as his power of attorney. We notarized an advance directive[101] to preplan in the event of another episode. Joe's brain would need rest and time to recover. It wasn't physiologically possible for him to function as I expected.

He apologized to my family for causing me such agony. They all showed him compassion, but it took time to rebuild trust. Two more grandchildren were born, and they all came to visit again. They enjoyed tractor rides, bonfires, and tire swing adventures.

Joe and my family partnered together and surprised me on my sixtieth birthday. Our friend Marcia was there. She and I had danced at each other's parties and hung out on occasional lunch dates. Through our friendship, we both danced right into the arms of our husbands.

She and Donald got married a couple of years after Joe and me. I was a little jealous of her fairy-tale wedding. It was a grand event at St. Peter and Paul's Basilica, in Chattanooga.[102] They were surrounded by family, friends, and our dance community.

Joe and I were among the prelude of couples who waltzed down the aisle to welcome the bride. Marcia was stunning in her white tea-length dress and flowers in her hair. Her elegance dazzled guests. Her military-uniformed son walked her down the aisle to give her away. I wished my four had come to my wedding. The violinist played an instrumental version of Celine Dion's "My Heart Will Go On."[103]

The "something borrowed" on her wedding day was my cream-colored lace shawl—perfect for her November wedding day walk from the church to the dance reception.

Marcia and Donald's dancing never slowed down even though mine and Joe's decreased to once a month. I never saw Marcia tired.

---

101 An advance directive is a document that helps patients preplan their treatment when they're unable to make conscious decisions about their healthcare: https://www.nia.nih.gov/health/advance-care-planning-healthcare-directives.

102 https://www.stspeterandpaulbasilica.com

103 Although Taylor Davis didn't play for Marcia and Donald's wedding, she gives us a feel for the rendition of "My Heart Will Go On." These four minutes are worth absorbing: https://www.youtube.com/watch?v=tFdlhlmQ-ek.

It wasn't only Joe's symptoms that hid before the life-threatening illness presented itself. Marcia's symptoms hid beneath her strong, healthy body, delaying the diagnosis. She wasn't feeling her best at my birthday party. Then two months later she confirmed the diagnosis of cancer. I assured her of my prayers and determined to be there to cheer her on in her battle. I left a phone message the day she planned treatment in Nashville. I had been hoping to hear her voice, and for her to be encouraged by mine.

Instead of hearing back from Marcia, I got a text from Donald. "Please come to the hospital to say goodbye."

I called Joe. "Meet me at the hospital," I said through my tears. "Marcia is dying." I could barely speak.

We met in the hospital parking lot. We hugged and cried and dried our tears before walking the long hallways with doors that didn't need to be locked.

She leaned on Donald's shoulder while he held her in the hospital bed. She couldn't respond, but we believed she heard us. Joe and I stayed by her side, loving, watching, and praying along with her family.

Marcia and I must have been soul sisters all this time. In those five hours of saying goodbye, her sons became my sons. Her sister and brother became my siblings. We listened. We watched. We waited.

Joe brought a playlist of gentle waltzes to ease the tension. He figured Donald needed soft music to aid his grief. After a few numbers, Donald said to Joe, "Are slow waltzes all you have? Marcia's favorites are faster foxtrots and swings. Do you have Elton John's 'Crocodile Rock'[104] or Frank Sinatra's 'Come Fly with Me'?"[105]

The hospital bed became Marcia and Donald's dance floor. Her breathing seemed calmer and more rhythmic while he held her with

---

104 "Crocodile Rock," https://www.youtube.com/watch?v=xw0EozkBWuI.
105 "Come Fly with Me," https://www.youtube.com/watch?v=HmQq6yLe2ww.

the music. The hours ticked by with this energetic showcase of foxtrots, sambas, and swings—and a few faster waltzes.

We watched Marcia dance from the arms of her husband into the arms of Jesus. Through tears, we could imagine her angelic figure with a flowing white gown. She was twirling through the streets of gold.

This divine invitation showed Joe and me how to dance differently. Marcia and Donald gave us that sacred space. We became aware of the delicate soul of our relationship. It was still risky. We needed to learn how to be intentional.

Chapter 28

DANCE OF CYCLES

Dance is your pulse, your heartbeat, your breathing. It's the
rhythm of your life. It's the expression in time and movement, in
happiness, joy, sadness, and envy.
—Jacques d'Amboise

L ittle did I know of the mental health benefits I derived from certain practices that had become well-worn neuropathways in my brain. For example, I quoted this verse on my college graduation day. I memorized it and resurrected it throughout the seasons of my life:

Finally, brethren, whatever things are true, whatever things
are noble, whatever things are just, whatever things are pure,
whatever things are lovely, whatever things are of good report,

if there is any virtue and if there is anything praise-worthy,
meditate on these things.[106]

Then I discovered through Gottman's research that healthy couples are gentle with each other before discussing a conflict. And the ratio of positive to negative interactions is five to one.[107] Also, Dr. Rick Hanson writes and speaks from a neuroscience perspective on how we can be aware of positive neuroplasticity.[108] Thoughts such as fear, negativity, and resentment naturally stick like Velcro on the brain's cells. And unless you ponder for fifteen seconds, positive thoughts on those same cells will slide off like Teflon.[109]

That's why it's important to consider things that are noble, pure, and lovely. Listening to inspirational music and visiting art museums are good for our mental well-being. Hanging out with positive and encouraging peers helps develop a positive bias that becomes a cushion of comfort and hope when life's difficulties happen.

Although our positive thinking can get us through hard times, it's vital not to be caught up in being too overly optimistic. Rather than ignore issues, we also must face brutal facts to recognize divine invitations to our authentic selves. The Stockdale paradox was named after a US admiral who survived eight years of captivity. Unlike many other prisoners of war, he balanced his optimism with the brutal reality of his torture, which was a key factor in his survival.[110]

---

106 Philippians 4:8
107 Level One Clinical Training; this information is in several of Gottman's books.
108 Neuroplasticity is the brain's capacity for change throughout the lifespan. This scholarly article gives more insight: https://www.ncbi.nlm.nih.gov/pmc/articles/PMC4960264/.
109 This three-minute video is a summary of Hanson's explanation: https://www.youtube.com/user/drrhanson.
110 This website sums up the Stockdale paradox: https://ndoherty.com/stockdale-paradox/.

We couldn't work on the marriage yet. Joe's year of sluggish depression was music to my achievement dance. I left the group practice of ten years, rebranded, and wrote blog articles. My speaking engagements and community involvement attracted leaders to my counseling practice. Marcia showed me the brevity of life. Joe needed recovery. But I needed growth.

> "Although our positive thinking can get us through hard times, it's vital not to be caught up in being too overly optimistic. Rather than ignore issues, we also must face brutal facts to recognize divine invitations to our authentic selves."

Two years later our couple's therapist normalized our issues. But I was concerned over Joe's exaggerations of his interactions with me. I feared the same demise as with my first marriage. At times I couldn't tell the difference between Joe and his illness. Our synchronized intensity/irritation dances made that differentiation more than difficult. Here are some examples:

Joe: Now let me have your attention.

Me: Hold on. (I was hyperfocused on writing a blog post)

Joe: (irritated and demanding) I need to tell you now while it's on my mind. I have other things to do. Now listen.

Me: Is this necessary now?

Joe: Yes, it is. Now listen. (He takes ten or twenty minutes to explain)

Me: Can we talk about this later? I don't need this now.

Joe: You interrupted me. It wouldn't take this long if you just listened the first time. Now what I said... (Then he would "teach me" how to respond.)

Even a simple visit to the food bar at a Chinese restaurant triggered his intensity and my confusion.

"Here, try this." He offered a shrimp on the end of his fork.

"No. I'm not interested."

"You could have said 'no thank you.' You need to be open to new things. Shrimp is good for you."

"Shrimp is not a new thing. I'm choosing not to eat it."

When I got up to get another plate of food, he examined what I chose. "You need more vegetables. That's so unhealthy."

If he won't listen to me while in his right mind, how could we possibly survive another episode? I wrote this phrase repeatedly in my prayer journals. I verbalized it several times over to Joe, our couple's therapist, and his individual therapist.

I wrote blogs about verbal abuse and mind games. I started believing that Joe was either unwilling or unable to empathize with me. I researched the relationship dances of empathic women with narcissistic men.[111] Had I been sucked into this dance without realizing it in my first marriage? Was that Joe's and my pattern? This was not just recovery from bipolar and psychotic episodes. I needed to change my part of the dance.

I enrolled in an eight-week mindfulness-based stress reduction course.[112] My regular practice of mindfulness helped me detach from the toxic dances. I couldn't convince Joe to be aware. But I could increase my awareness.

Since my first spiritual direction retreat, I had established patterns for my soul care. I recharged about every ninety days. It coincided with the waves of tension in our marriage. After each getaway, Joe greeted me in the driveway and we dialogued about my experiences. Our relationship got smoother until the need for another retreat three months later.

Those regular Pilgrimage Altar experiences helped me return to the dim cottage of my marriage. I still met God in desperation, looking for His divine invitations.

111 Lisa A. Romano and Kim Saeed are life coaches raising our awareness about narcissistic abuse. See lisaaromano.com & kimsaeed.com.

112 Mindfulness-based stress reduction not only increases awareness but also contributes to physical and mental wellness on several levels: https://www. umassmed.edu/cfm/mindfulness-based-programs/mbsr-courses/about-mbsr/ history-of-mbsr/.

I stayed in the apartment of the retreat center's main building,[113] on the second floor overlooking Tennessee's Cumberland Plateau. Natural light from the large windows created a perfect analogy to my Canada retreat.

This time I sought clarity for my book. I spread out manuscripts and journals to inventory my writing before Joe's episode. But since then, other stressors interfered. My mother-in-law passed away. Joe discovered major calcification on his heart. We changed to a whole-foods, plant-based diet.

After my three-day retreat, I felt clear and motivated. I gathered my manuscripts and journals and arrived home. Joe was disheveled, having rearranged furniture and worked on major projects. "Now don't say anything yet," he said. "Let me show you around before you come to conclusions. I thought a lot about this, and I know I'm right. I've spent hours figuring this out. I don't want you to judge it; just be open."

"You don't have to convince me, Joe. I'm okay," I said. He took me around the house.

"I've studied this in my mind, and I know what I'm doing. I'm the best."

When we settled, I told him about my retreat and asked about our church service.

"I didn't go. I had my own retreat away from you. I stayed up late because it felt good."

"How late?"

"I don't know. About three o'clock."

"I'm surprised you'd stay up till then."

"I stayed up because I wanted to. I know how to take care of myself. I can do what I want." He trailed off in his usual long lectures.

---

113 Saint Mary's Retreat Center is located in Sewanee, Tennessee: https://www.stmaryssewanee.org.

I listened calmly. All the signs were there. If those same interactions were in another marriage or in another man, it may not have mattered. But it did matter. Grandiosity, irritability, negative thinking, little sleep, mentally sluggish.

The next day he listened to my concerns and assured me of his awareness. "I'm okay. I promise." And I believed him. Although I didn't imagine another episode, I wrote in my journal:

> I know we're not out of the woods yet, Lord. Yesterday didn't take me so off guard. I no longer fear. I'm more aware. Lord, please help Joe see in himself what I see. We need that couple's appointment sooner than later.

Five days later, Joe drove me, my adult daughter, and granddaughter to the Mother's Day church service. It was my youngest granddaughter's baby dedication. I cherished our thirty-minute ride to the church. That was the best Mother's Day gift I could receive, being with my daughter and granddaughter.

But Joe was nervous about finding the church. I worried because it was the same town as the marriage conference that became a prelude to his mania less than three years before. When we arrived, I felt uneasy.

A greeter said, "Happy Mother's Day."

"Thank you."

A few feet behind me, Joe said, "Did you wish her Happy Mother's Day?"

I looked back, embarrassed. "He just said that to me."

Then he smiled and shook hands with the male greeter. "Have a Happy Mother's Day yourself!" He was as high as Jim Carey's character in *The Truman Show*.[114]

---

114 *The Truman Show* movie trailer: https://www.youtube.com/watch?v=loTIzXAS7v4.

We sat five rows from the front. Richard and his wife, a fellow cheerleader in college, sat behind us. All grandparents, little cousins, aunts, and uncles sat together.

Oh, Lord, please help Joe calm down.

My heart beat faster when we held hands as the service began. Joe's were cold and sweaty. We sang and swayed to the rhythm of three violinists leading worship. His tearful emotions looked like a normal movement of the Holy Spirit. But I knew better. Then he left for the bathroom. He came back when the service was over.

"I was worried about you. Are you all right?"

"I'm fine," he said. "I didn't want to hear a boring sermon. I talked to the deacons. They prayed for me. One of them knows you from counseling."

Oh my gosh. What did he share? Do I ask Richard to take our daughter and granddaughter home?

Joe was less nervous, and the girls didn't notice. After we dropped them off and arrived home, he said to me, "Let's talk on the front porch."

After we settled on the porch, he said, "Now I don't want you to be alarmed. But I need to check into the hospital tonight. I'm not feeling right, and there've been a lot of changes in my diet. They'll check my medications."

"What if you don't meet criteria for inpatient?"

"Oh, I'll qualify. Don't worry about that. I want you to call the hospital and let them know I'm coming."

"Okay, I can drive you there."

"No." He got more agitated, so I stopped my questions. "I'll drive myself. Trust me. I will go on my own. I'll text you when I get there. But when I get admitted, I won't have my phone. I need to get away from you. I feel too stressed."

"Okay." I called the hospital. But Joe waited another three hours before leaving our driveway. As promised, he texted when he got there.

The next evening, he walked through our front door.

"I'm surprised you're home this early," I said. "I was getting ready to call the hospital."

"STOP. I don't want to hear about the hospital. I just waited in line for an hour for my prescription. It's not covered by insurance. Just get away from me."

How could this be? I had just gotten back from a retreat. Joe had no stressors from me like he did before. He persuaded me that he was fine. I believed him. *He went thirteen years without an episode. This is his second within our short marriage of eight years. The marriage is making him sick.*[115]

It was like the movie *Groundhog Day*.[116] I presented a workshop while Joe waited in the ER forty-eight hours before police transport to a different psychiatric hospital. Three days later he didn't fit criteria for mandatory treatment. Instead of a family meeting at the hospital, I testified before the judge. Others present included the psychiatrist, hospital director, social worker, Joe, and his attorney. In our case, the advance directive became a useless document unacknowledged by the hospital system.

"Your honor, I cannot assure my husband's safety if he's discharged today. His illness puts him in danger to himself and others. His last episode caused a near-death auto accident. He cannot come home."

"I object, your honor," the attorney said. "The testimony from the previous episode doesn't describe this one."

The judge spoke. "Mrs. Herman, can you give us specifics about the current episode?"

---

115 My therapists and others remind me that "the marriage is making him sick" is an irrational thought. Psychosis and bipolar disorders are not so simple that one can make such conclusions. Yet the rational (left) hemisphere of the brain wants answers.

116 *Groundhog Day* movie is about a man who wakes up living the same day several times over until he becomes aware and intentional for change. Here's the movie trailer: https://www.youtube.com/watch?v=tSVeDx9fk60.

"Yes." And I repeated the list of symptoms. The look on everyone's face made it clear to me that my list didn't meet criteria for mandatory treatment.

The judge said, "Mrs. Herman, I'm sorry. But these current symptoms don't indicate that your husband is in danger to himself or others."

I tried speaking through the lump in my throat, and I couldn't stop my tears. "You don't understand. His poor judgment is a major part of his illness. He WILL be in danger to himself if you discharge him today. He had two hospitalizations with a near-death accident in between! HE ALMOST DIED. I CAN'T ensure his safety! DOESN'T THAT MATTER?"

Joe teared up while others around the conference table bowed their heads.

His psychiatrist tried to negotiate. "Joe, if you stayed another day or two, you'd be more stable."

"I can't get sleep here. I'll get better at home."

I was impressed with his psychiatrist. But I hated the hospital system. I had no other choice than to drive him home. I stayed with my parents and presented another workshop that evening.

The delusions were just as intense but lasted three weeks instead of six. One morning at my mom and stepdad's, I felt nauseous. I packed up and quickly left without saying goodbye. I headed straight for the bedroom and doubled over in a fetal position on the bed. Tears and groans flooded uncontrollably.

"Can I get you anything?" Joe asked.

"No, I need rest." He closed the curtains and the door. I needed the rest like I had in that cottage in Canada.

When I calmed, the darkness was gone. I felt no sorrow. But I felt free. Our couple's therapist didn't agree with my idea to separate, but we all three agreed to call it a "sabbatical." My individual therapist said to me, "Judy, you have phenomenal staying power." Then she looked me in the eyes and said firmly, "That's not a compliment."

I talked with my friend Lisa about whether I should follow through with a sabbatical or not.

"Judy, I notice your body tense up when you talk about staying with Joe."

"Really?"

"But when you talk about a sabbatical, your body is relaxed."

"You noticed that?"

"Yes, I did. I think you're done."

I paused. "You're right. I just don't want to admit it."

Penny said, "Judy, I don't think you're done, but I think you're resolved." She agreed with my friend. Somehow the phrase "you're done" sounded angry. I wasn't angry or done. I was resolved.

My body, my friends, and my therapist saw the truth.

Chapter 29

DANCE OF A MESSY RELATIONSHIP

We dance for laughter, we dance for tears, we dance for madness, we dance for fears, we dance for hopes, we dance for screams, we are the dancers, we create the dreams.
—Albert Einstein

I stayed at our missionary friends' home while they traveled for a month. Each evening I walked in Karen's neighborhood and occasionally visited with her neighbors. I did my own grocery shopping and cooked meals in her kitchen. I looked at pictures of her family and noticed how much her presence was in her home. Then I wondered, *How much is my presence in our home?* I thought of Joe's overpowering personality. I decorated my office the way he suggested. I trusted my preferences less when I was with him. Was my home a reflection of my authentic self? Had I lost myself catering to his illness, recovery, and persuasion dance? Had I misaligned with who I really am?

After three weeks, I came back to the master bedroom while Joe slept in his room. Our sleep cycles never aligned. But it didn't matter anymore.

I was aware like I never had been before. Social engineering didn't work in either marriage. Handwritten love letters in brown hardback journals weren't taken to heart. Nor did the one in the red envelope from decades before. But I could still dance to the rhythm of life. And if there was another shattered cup, I'd pick up the pieces and craft a beautiful mosaic. I'd be intentional to listen for the change in music. Whether they were slow and comforting waltzes or faster foxtrots, I'd catch my breath in between and allow fresh air to permeate my soul. Then I'd take the hand of the nice-looking man and dance along with the Father, Son, and Holy Spirit. I could risk remembering and forgiving. I had peace in my heart whether or not Joe and I could align with divine invitations for a new marriage. All I knew was that I couldn't go back to the old one. That's why our sleep cycles and separate bedrooms didn't matter anymore.

For a few days, we followed national news about the upcoming eclipse of the sun. Its shadow path would travel across the entire continent with spectacular views close to our home. This once-in-a-lifetime phenomenon would show us the total eclipse if we traveled an hour north.

We watched documentaries, Googled animations, times, locations, and forecasts. But uncertain weather would determine our disappointment or exhilaration. A multitude of others intended to travel farther away with unpredictable traffic. We routed back roads and small towns to avoid congested highways. We intended to start out early with plenty of margin to find the best place to look up with our eclipse glasses. Traffic, cloud cover, and weather were factors we couldn't control.

Even though hotels, Airbnbs, and campsites were sold out, on a whim I said to Joe, "Why don't we check out some campgrounds?

Would you call and find out if anyone has any sites open?" It was more than unlikely. But it didn't hurt to ask.

"Oh, there won't be anything open at this point," he said.

"Well, what do we have to lose if we try? Isn't it best to know than not know?"

He called some privately owned campgrounds in the path of totality. He left several messages to different places, not expecting return calls.

One person called back with one campsite available. We prepared our Pack N Play. Then we loaded bicycles on the back of our white Xterra along with our red Mohawk canoe. Since taking several trips a year, our system was efficient.

"I'm surprised you wanted to camp," he said. Our lives were misaligned. We didn't know if the marriage was sustainable.

"Yeah, I don't mind," I said. Then I thought, *Why should we let our grievances keep us from experiencing such a rare cosmic phenomenon?*

We checked in at the camp office and followed a nine-year-old boy on his bicycle to the gravel driveway of our site. The boy showed us the utility hookups, oriented us to the bathhouse, and asked if we needed anything. Our site was the last one, just a few feet from the lake under the open sky. It was more than we anticipated.

We felt the energy and laughter of a Girl Scout troop next to us. One of the dads set up a high-powered telescope on a sturdy tripod. Three guys in their early twenties from Vermont played their guitars. Families with young children, dogs, and older people with massive RVs filled the campground. Foreign accents and different languages made us feel we'd traveled far. But it was only an hour away.

"Do we want to see it from our canoe?" I asked, wondering if we'd feel too unstable. "It may be best to feel grounded while aligned with the earth, moon, and sun."

"I don't know," Joe said. "We could stay right here and experience it with other people."

With our eclipse glasses on, we saw the moon take a bite out of the sun. Time ticked slowly until the sun became like a crescent moon, yet still as bright as daylight. As more people gathered around our open space, we decided to watch from the lake.

We hopped in our faithful red canoe and paddled to the spot we scouted earlier that day. Joe grabbed the rope with anchor attached. Just as he lowered it, another boater's loud country music intruded on our peace across the water.

"I can't believe this," I said to Joe, laughing. "It's almost sacrilegious."

Just moments later, the music stopped.

Hundreds of campers and visitors outlined our space as if we were a small detail of a large framed picture. We felt connected to the other boaters.

The cloudless blue sky transformed into a calm darkness as if a storm were about to erupt.

Night fell in seconds, and the crowd began to cheer. The sliver of sun disappeared, and we took off our glasses. We gasped in disbelief.

"Oh my gosh.

"Oh my, I can't believe it.

"Oh my. This is amazing." The rest of what we said was speechless.

We couldn't take our eyes off the gold ring with three magical rays from the sun's corona. It felt like an angelic being, but it was God's gift of love to the two of us and hundreds of our closest friends.

Those two-and-a-half minutes stood still as we took one last glance at the diamond ring finale. Then, while we faced each other on opposite sides of the canoe, we both reached for the other's hand. The canoe rocked, and we laughed through our warm tears. We held tight to each other. But we didn't tip over. Instead, through weather and space, we felt aligned like never before.

EPILOGUE

Since watching the eclipse of the sun, I've started many mornings going outside to look up. I have a new respect for the moon and stars when it's clear in the morning. Even when it's cloudy I take time to look up. God reminds me to be aware of divine invitations.

With all the years of journal and diary writing, I never imagined writing a published book. This writing project was my intentional therapy after Joe's last episode eighteen months ago. My first very rough draft took shape in the fall of 2017. Then on March 1, 2018, I risked opening up to my beta readers on a closed Facebook group. That was the same day I answered a frantic call from my mom. Her and my stepdad, Bob, had just arrived home from their music class with lighthearted laugher and fun with their friends. But during the call, he died suddenly in her presence.

I came to believe that Marcia and Bob had shown me the brevity of life. And it seemed both were telling me to write these messages from my heart to yours.

The writing, rewriting, deletions, and edits of this book became my sacred space. Most days before I wrote, I walked outside, and looked up. Then I said out loud, "Here I am, Lord. Thanks for meeting me. Show me what to write."

I researched, indexed, and cataloged four decades of handwritten journals. I laughed and cried during some of my forgotten stories. Others were boring. And some were embarrassing or outright emotionally draining to read. But one journal inspired me from cover to cover. It was the one from my spiritual direction retreat in Canada.

My writing coach and structural editor said, "Don't share your manuscript with anyone whom you depend on, live under the same roof with, or have sex with. Not until you're done, of course." So, I took her advice. The week before my publisher meeting, Joe began to read. As he read the last scenes of the manuscript, I sat across from him doing case notes on my laptop. I was aware of his every nuance and gesture.

"Are you all right?" I asked.

"I'm fine. Please don't worry about me. I'll let you know when I'm finished."

"Okay." I was still uneasy.

A few minutes later he said, "I'm done."

"Oh?"

"Yes. I'm proud of you, Judy. It wasn't easy to read. But I'm at peace with what you wrote. Nothing in your story is a surprise. We've talked about everything here. There's just more color to it in your written words."

"Oh? You're okay with what I wrote?"

"Yes. I know it will touch a lot of people's lives. This is an extension of our ministry. Of course, I can't read it objectively because I'm your husband. But it's your story and it's our story. I live with the darkness of my illness every day. I grieve to know I've caused you pain. I knew that before reading the book. And you know that I forgive myself. And like you said, we all need to forgive and remember."

I took a deep breath and teared up. We felt aligned in this project just as we did on the canoe watching the eclipse. Writing this book has reminded me of the rope attached to the anchor of our relationship.

Our messy relationships with the family have transformed into gathering together for the grandchildren's birthday parties. Mine and Richard's marriage was not a failure after twenty-nine years. Not only do we share grandchildren, but our two sons and two daughters have also become aunts, uncles, parents, and spouses.

This book has helped me appreciate trials more than I could have otherwise. We all can forgive and remember. But it's not easy in the moment. And sometimes even years later. What I've written are my experiences and meanings. My prayer is that I didn't contribute to my or anyone else's shame by silence, secrecy, or judgment. Instead, I want to honor the authentic journey.

For those who read these words who have been harmed by me and my lack of awareness or judgment, I say to you, "I'm sorry." May your reading this book be an offering of laying down my little white rose. And may we both stand up together and look up in gratitude to God for the struggle of our humanity. May we remember His forgiveness as we forgive ourselves and others.

My intentions throughout this writing have been to honor each person and relationship. From the unnamed homeschooling

Photo by Neelu Eldurkar

acquaintance to my most intimate relationships, I say, "Thank you." Each person has joined hands with God and has been a mirror to my soul. Maybe this book has been a mirror for you too.

As we breathe AIR in and out of our bodies and souls, let's thank God for both wise and unwise risks. May we be more aware and intentional for the risks we need to take toward becoming our authentic selves.

This book and its messages could not have been written without my beloved Joe. Our irritation/reaction dance still shows up at times. We're working on mastering the resilience/growth dance. We both have great rhythm and timing. God may be changing the music for us. And, for now, we're still dancing.

ACKNOWLEDGMENTS

First of all, I thank my loving heavenly Father who has invited me into the sacred spaces of my written prayers. From my ten-year-old diary to my current journal writing, I thank You for mixing Holy Scriptures with the ink of my tears and belly laughs of my soul.

To my clients, I say thank you for entrusting me with your journey. Your courage has given me determination to write this book. I appreciate how you've shown me your struggles and resilience.

To my structural editor and writing coach, Marion Roach Smith, I say a huge thanks. From our first one-on-one lunchtime at Jeff Goin's Tribe Conference, I resonated with you. After I nearly memorized your new Memoir Structure Class, I had a clear course of action. You helped me make my writing flow. Your wisdom made this process seem like therapy. Although I occasionally visited my therapist, I needed both your "therapy and guidance." And of course, I say thank you to my therapist, Pam Johnson, who has helped me with insights across the seasons of my life.

Thank you, Karen Anderson, for inviting me into the Morgan James Publishing family. I felt a kindred spirit with your marriage and family counselor background. Thank you, Aubrey Kosa, Margo Toulouse, Jim Howard, and David Hancock. You have guided me and listened. I thank you, Angie Kiesling. You made my writing voice more authentic with your line edits.

To my beta readers, I thank you for being the first group to entrust in this process. You read my messy manuscripts and shared your confusion, suggestions, and helpful critiques. You supported me through my struggle. I thank you, Alice Taylor. You were the first to be so vulnerable with your comments. I cried with gratitude as I read how you interacted with my writing. Laura McCoy, you've been one of my biggest cheerleaders among our Tribe Writer's groups. Cori Leigh, I love how you cheered for Joe in my story. I appreciate you, Justin Hockey. You resonated, a generation younger than me on the other side of the world. Jennifer Schlau, I thank you for your librarian expertise. I'm honored that you took the time to engage with my book amongst the many other books and authors you support. Thank you, Teresa Colon, Anita Idleman, Nancy Booth, and many others. You've supported me since my first plunge into showing my raw self in early drafts.

To other early readers and proofreaders, your eyes on my manuscript helped with fine-tuning. I say a big thanks to authors Tom Bakewell, J. L. Callison, Tom Dutta, and Natalie Eastman. Thank you to other proofreaders, including April Brobston, Tiffany Babb, Suzanne Burrell, Sheaba Cherian, Lisa Harris, Sheila Hoffman, Julianna Foster, and Nancy Wahler.

Thank you, Bill O'Hanlan, Michael Hyatt, and Jeff Goins for unveiling the mystery of this book-writing and publishing process for me. Thank you, Drs. John and Julie Gottman, Dr. Harville Hendrix, and Helen LaKelly Hunt for your training and helping me make sense of my messy relationships. Thank you, Dr. David G Benner, for transformational experiences as my Spiritual Director and professor. Writing those scenes from my journals has given me even more clarity over your impact in my story. I thank you, Dr. Dan Siegel, from our brief meeting to the lasting influence of your books and teaching. And I thank you, Dr. Brené Brown. Your messages of vulnerability and courage continue to impact me. I thank you, Fr. Richard Rohr. Along with your other books and teaching, the little book, *Just This,* was my daily inspiration while writing my manuscript.

I appreciate my uncle, Dr. Ken Idleman. Your influence permeates the seasons of my life. Thank you for giving me genuine feedback and encouragement after reading through my manuscript. You calmed my soul before the rest of my family read it.

Thanks to the three men who have shaped my passion. "Mark," even though we were young and ignorant, I'm thankful now for my determination to cherish and honor the gift of life. To "Richard," I say thank you for the four remarkable human beings who have shown me divine mother love. Thank you for shaping my mother heart, Candace, Carrie, Andrew, and Steven. And I thank each of my precious grandchildren. You've shown me a dimension of life and divine love bigger than my words can describe.

And to my life's dance partner, Joe, I say thank you, my love. At our age, neither of us knew we would birth a new being. But, out of the darkest times of our marriage, I became pregnant with *Beyond Messy Relationships.* While you recovered from the storm in your brain and felt the abandonment of our "sabbatical," you gave me space to write. Without a promise that I could stay, you knew I wouldn't go back to our familiar dances. When the shame of your recovery was at its peak, you chose to lean into my pain. My refusal to abort what's very much alive in my heart wasn't easy for you. I'll forever be grateful for the quality of man you are. You've joined hands with God to nurture and give life to this book. Your resilience and growth have changed the music of our marriage. I love you more than I ever have, my husband and best friend.

ABOUT THE AUTHOR

Judy K. Herman counsels those in leadership including entrepreneurs, clergy, and other therapists. As a counselor, writer and public speaker, she is also known as a soul cheerleader. As a licensed professional counselor and mental health service provider in Tennessee, she is also a National Certified Counselor who specializes in relationships. She has trained with world-renowned marriage experts. Her focus is on helping leaders and families create connection beyond conflict. In 2006, she began private practice with growing expertise in couples' counseling.

She writes articles addressing mental health, marriage, faith, and relationship well-being.

Along with writing and counseling, Judy facilitates individual and group retreats. She's delivered numerous speaking engagements at universities, churches, non-profit and civic organizations.

For fun, she and her husband enjoy outdoor activities. Camping, hiking, canoeing, and bike-riding are among them. They also enjoy their dancing. But most of all, it's the adventures with grandchildren that rank the highest!

HOW TO CONTACT JUDY

For more relationship help, check out additional resources.

Keynotes, Seminars, Workshops and Retreats

Invite Judy to speak at your next event. For details, you can contact her at judyspeaker.com. She addresses topics such as, conflict resolution, family relationships, spiritual formation, and leadership.

Connect through social media

facebook/JudyKHerman

twitter.com/JudyKHerman

linkedin.com/in/judykherman/

MessyRelationships.com

Download Free Resources

- Reflection chapter questions for insights on your story
- List of feeling words and defensive behaviors
- Relationship Stress Test
- … and so much more!

Share your messy relationship success stories at MessyRelationships.com

Printed in the USA
CPSIA information can be obtained
at www.ICGtesting.com
JSHW022320140824
68134JS00019B/1207

9 781642 793215